Foundations of NLP: Simplified for Beginners

Understanding Natural Language Processing with Machine Learning and Deep Learning Concepts

by

Dr. Khushboo Shah

This book is dedicated to my teachers

Prof. (Dr.) Hiren Joshi & Prof. (Dr.) Hardik Joshi,

whose encouragement and belief in my knowledge inspired me to write this book.

PREFACE

Welcome to the world of Natural Language Processing (NLP)! In today's digital age, where vast amounts of text data are generated every second, understanding and processing human language has become more crucial than ever. Whether it's improving search engine results, automating customer support, or extracting insights from social media posts, NLP plays a pivotal role in numerous applications that shape our daily lives.

This book is designed as an introductory guide to NLP for beginners and students. Our aim is to simplify the complex world of NLP and provide you with a solid foundation to explore this fascinating field further. Whether you're a curious student eager to delve into the fields of machine learning and artificial intelligence or a professional looking to expand your skill set, this book will equip you with the fundamental concepts and techniques of NLP.

We start by laying the groundwork with an exploration of basic NLP concepts, including text preprocessing, parts of speech tagging, and named entity recognition. As we progress, we explore statistical methods and machine learning techniques commonly used in NLP, such as language models, TF-IDF, and neural networks. Through clear explanations and practical examples, you'll gain insight into how these methods can be applied to real-world problems.

In addition to covering essential NLP techniques, we also discuss advanced topics such as deep learning models, sentiment analysis, and ethical considerations in NLP. By the end of this book, you'll have a solid understanding of the core principles of NLP and the tools and techniques used to process and analyse human language.

It's worth noting that NLP is a rapidly evolving field, with new research and advancements emerging regularly. While this book provides a comprehensive introduction to NLP concepts, we encourage you to continue exploring, experimenting, and learning from additional resources to stay updated with the latest developments.

Whether you're beginning a journey of self-discovery or seeking to enhance your professional skills, we hope this book serves as a valuable resource in your quest to understand the fascinating world of Natural Language Processing.

Happy learning!
Prof.(Dr.)Khushboo Shah

List of Figures

Figure 1: NLP - Fusion of AI, CS and Human Language 1

Figure 2:Techniques and methodologies of language processing systems 13

Figure 3: Text acquisition from various sources 19

Figure 4: Stop words removal process 23

Figure 5: Word2Vec Representation 74

Figure 6: CBOW vs. SKIPGRAM 75

Figure 7: FastText center word embedding 82

Figure 8: BERT Model 86

Figure 9: Machine Learning Algorithms Classification 101

Figure 10: Supervised Machine Learning Model 103

Figure 11: Unsupervised Machine Learning Model 107

Figure 12: Semi-Supervised Machine Learning Model 111

Figure 13: Reinforcement Learning Example 114

Figure 14: Logistic Regression 121

Figure 15: Support Vector Machine 125

Figure 16: Decision Tree 134

Figure 17: Random Forest 141

Figure 18: K- Nearest Neighbour 149

Figure 19: Binary Classification vs. Multiclass Classification ... 154

Figure 20: (a)One-vs-One (b) One-vs-All 156

Figure 21: DL-ML-NLP-AI all connected with each other 161

Figure 22: Human brain network vs. Artificial neural network .. 163

Figure 23: Artificial Neural Network Layers 164

List of Tables

Table 1: Evolution stages of NLP 9
Table 2: Word Stemming 26
Table 3:Lemmatization technique 30
Table 4: Common POS tags 33
Table 5: NER Examples 36
Table 6: Samples of text normalization 40
Table 7: Normalization on numerical data 42
Table 8: Junk data removal examples 45
Table 9: Spell checking and correction 48
Table 10: One hot encoding 53
Table 11: Word embedding examples 54
Table 12: Vectorization with TFIDF 56
Table 13: Encoding vs. Vectorization 58
Table 14: GPT Evolution 96

Table of Contents

1 Introduction to Natural Language Processing 1

1.1 What is NLP? 3

1.2 Why is NLP important? 4

1.3 Applications of NLP in everyday life 5

1.4 The Evolution of NLP 8

1.5 The Road Ahead 12

2 Fundamental Concepts of Text PreProcessing 13

2.1 What is Text PreProcessing 15

2.2 Text Acquisition 18

2.3 Tokenization 20

2.4 Stop Words Removal 22

2.5 Stemming 25

2.6 Lemmatization 29

2.7 Part-of-Speech Tagging 33

2.8 Named Entity Recognition 36

2.9 Normalization 39

2.10 Junk Data Removal 43

2.11 Spell Checking and Correction 46

2.12 Noise Reduction 49

2.13 Encoding and Vectorization 52

2.13.1 One-Hot Encoding 52

2.13.2 Word Embeddings 54

2.13.3 Vectorization with TF-IDF 55

3 Statistical Methods in NLP 60
3.1 Introduction to probability and statistics in NLP 61
3.1.1 Probability in NLP 61
3.1.2 Statistics in NLP 62
3.2 TF-IDF 68
3.3 Advanced Word Embedding Techniques 73
3.3.1 Word2Vec 73
3.3.2 GloVe 75
3.3.3 FastText 81
3.3.4 BERT 85
3.3.5 GPT 91
3.3.6 XLNet 97
4 Machine Learning Basics 100
4.1 Types of ML Algorithms 102
4.1.1 Supervised learning 102
4.1.2 Unsupervised learning 106
4.1.3 Semi-supervised learning 110
4.1.4 Reinforcement learning 113
4.2 Machine Learning Classifiers 119
4.2.1 Logistic Regression 121
4.2.2 Support Vector Machine 124
4.2.3 Naive Bayes 130
4.2.4 Decision Tree 132
4.2.5 Random Forest 140
4.2.6 K-Nearest Neighbours 145

4.2.7 Other Binary Classifiers 153

4.2.8 Multi-Class Classifiers 153

5 Deep Learning for NLP 161

5.1 Introduction to Neural Networks 162

5.2 Recurrent Neural Networks and Long Short-Term Memory Networks 165

5.3 Convolutional Neural Networks 168

5.4 Sequence-to-Sequence Models 170

5.5 Transfer Learning 171

5.6 Evaluation Metrics 173

5.7 Applications of Deep Learning in NLP 174

5.8 Challenges and Future Direction 176

6 Practical Applications 179

6.1 Sentiment analysis 180

6.1.1 Methodologies of Sentiment analysis 181

6.1.2 Applications of Sentiment analysis 182

6.2 Classifications 184

6.2.1 Text classification 184

6.2.2 Binary Classification 184

6.2.3 Topic Classification 185

6.2.4 Multiclass Classification 186

6.2.5 Named Entity Recognition 187

7 Ethical Considerations in NLP 190

7.1 Bias and fairness in NLP algorithms 191

7.2 Privacy concerns and data protection 193

8 Handson Practice 196
8.1 Text preprocessing on string 196
8.2 Spelling Correction and Normalization 202
8.3 Number extraction and NER on string 204
8.4 Binary classification of movie reviews 205
8.5 Multiclass classification on set of words 210
9 NLP Practical Exercises 214
10 Common Terms 219
11 Common Python Libraries 224
12 Hundred Comprehensive Questions on NLP 226

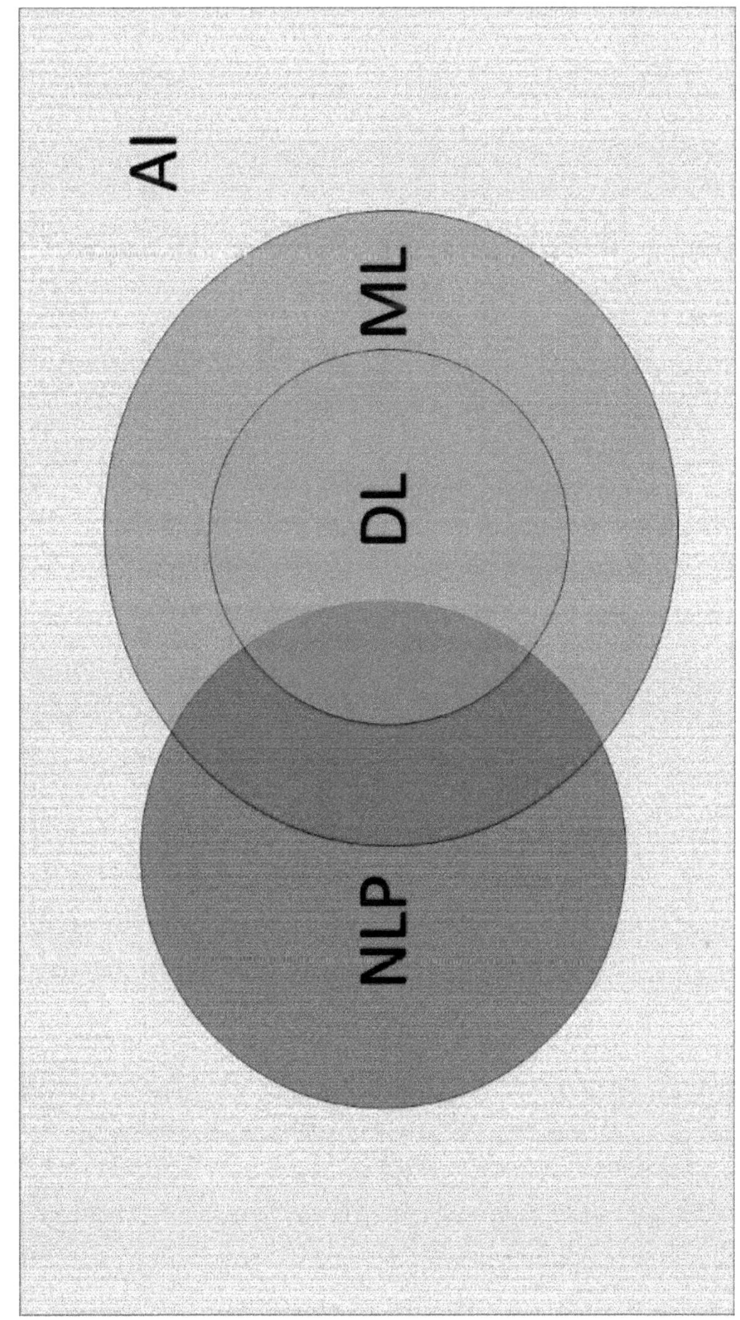
AI
ML
DL
NLP

1 Introduction to Natural Language Processing

Natural Language Processing (NLP) serves as a captivating fusion of computer science, artificial intelligence, and linguistics, offering a gateway to understand the mysteries of human language through computational means. In an era defined by the exponential growth of digital information and the omnipresence of communication technologies, the study of NLP has emerged as a cornerstone for understanding and harnessing the power of language in the digital age. At its core, NLP endeavours to bridge the gap between human communication and machine understanding, enabling computers to comprehend, interpret, and generate natural language text and speech.

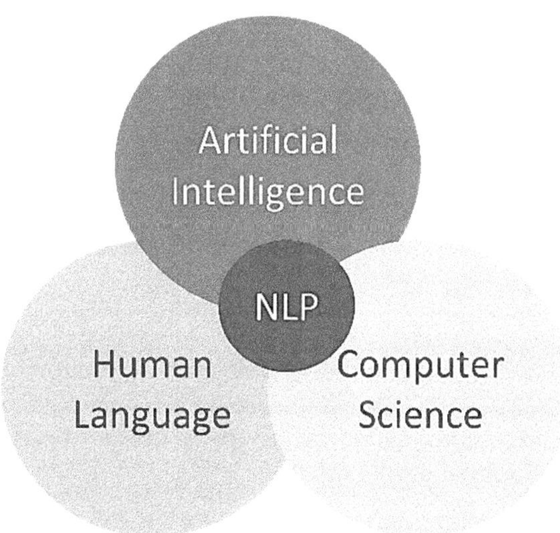

Figure 1: NLP - Fusion of AI, CS and Human Language

History of NLP

- 1940s-1950s: Early foundations laid in machine translation.
- 1950s-1960s: Emergence of the term "Natural Language Processing"; exploration of computational linguistics and parsing techniques.
- 1960s-1970s: Development of formal grammars and parsing algorithms; emphasis on syntax and semantics.
- 1980s-1990s: Rise of statistical approaches with techniques like Hidden Markov Models (HMMs) and probabilistic context-free grammars (PCFGs).
- Late 1990s-Early 2000s: Advent of the internet leads to exploration of data-driven methods and robust parsing.
- 2000s-Present: Deep learning revolutionizes NLP with neural network architectures like RNNs, CNNs, and Transformers.
- Recent Developments: Advancements in large-scale pretraining models such as GPT, BERT, and RoBERTa push the boundaries of language understanding and generation.

In this chapter, we start a journey into the captivating knowledge of NLP, where we thoroughly explore its foundations, significance, and numerous applications that permeate various facets of modern life. NLP has undergone a remarkable evolution. It started with humble beginnings rooted in rule-based systems and handcrafted linguistic rules. Today, it is characterized by cutting-edge deep learning models and neural language processing. This evolution has been fueled by advances in technology and computational linguistics.

As we explore the details of NLP, we will explain its basic concepts. We will look at how it is used in different fields. We will also think about the ethical issues and challenges that come with its fast progress. This chapter is for everyone. Whether you are a curious student wanting to learn about artificial intelligence or a professional looking to improve your language processing skills, this chapter will help you. It will show you how NLP can change the future of human-computer interaction and information processing.

1.1 What is NLP?

Natural Language Processing (NLP) combines technology and linguistics. NLP helps machines understand, interpret, and use human language. This is hard because language is complex, with ambiguity, context-dependency, and nuanced structures. Unlike programming languages with strict rules, human language is dynamic and multifaceted. This makes it challenging for computers to analyze. NLP uses methods like statistical modeling, machine learning, and computational linguistics. These methods help decode language and enable smooth interaction between humans and machines.

NLP, or Natural Language Processing, is really important because it's used in many things, we do every day. Think about search engines like Google, Siri or Alexa, language translation apps, and tools that understand how we feel from what we write online. NLP helps us find information, talk to our devices, and make decisions easier. Businesses use NLP to understand what people are saying online and get insights from it. Researchers use it to explore new topics, and regular people benefit by being able to talk to technology like they would to a person. As we have more and more text online, NLP becomes even more valuable because it helps us make sense of it all and use it to make smart choices.

1.2 Why is NLP important?

NLP is super important in today's digital world. With the internet and social media, there's a ton of text being shared online all the time. NLP helps us make sense of all this information by organizing it and finding the important stuff. It's like teaching computers to understand human language. This helps businesses make smart decisions using data, makes it easier for customers to get what they need, and sparks new ideas in lots of different fields. NLP is used everywhere, from healthcare to finance, education, and entertainment. It changes how we use technology and communicate with each other online.

NLP has important effects on accessibility and inclusion. It helps break down communication barriers and supports people with different language backgrounds. Language translation services, speech recognition systems, and text-to-speech technologies help cross-cultural communication. They also make information accessible to people with disabilities. By making technology more inclusive and accessible, NLP helps create a more fair and connected society. As NLP continues to advance, its potential for impact in many fields is huge. These fields include healthcare, personalized learning, content moderation, and crisis response.

1.3 Applications of NLP in everyday life

NLP is very versatile and used in many different fields. It changes how we interact with technology, access information, and make decisions. One main use of NLP is in search engines. NLP algorithms power search engines like Google. They analyze the meaning of search queries and web content to give relevant results. By understanding the context and intent behind search queries, NLP helps search engines provide more accurate and personalized responses. This improves the user experience and makes it easier to find information.

Machine translation is another amazing use of NLP. It helps bridge language gaps and encourages communication between different cultures. Services like Google Translate use NLP techniques to translate text automatically between languages. This lets people access information and communicate across language barriers. Whether translating web pages, documents, or real-time conversations, NLP-powered machine translation services help connect the world and share knowledge globally.

One example of NLP at work is machine translation, such as Google Translate. This technology translates text from one language to another. For example, if you have a sentence in English and want to understand it in your own language, machine translation can do that quickly. It's not always perfect, but it's improving in understanding and translating languages more accurately.

Text summarization is another useful use of NLP. It helps manage the overwhelming amount of information we encounter in the digital age. NLP algorithms can shorten long documents, articles, or conversations into brief summaries. They extract important insights and key information while keeping the original meaning intact. Whether creating executive summaries of research papers or brief recaps of news articles, text summarization tools using NLP improve efficiency and productivity by helping users understand complex content quickly.

Sentiment analysis is a powerful use of NLP. It helps understand public opinion, brand sentiment, and customer feedback. NLP algorithms analyze text to determine if it expresses positive, negative, or neutral feelings. This gives valuable insights to businesses, marketers, and policymakers. Whether tracking social media discussions, reviewing product feedback, or assessing customer satisfaction, sentiment analysis using NLP helps organizations make informed decisions and adjust strategies based on audience preferences. For example, if you review a movie saying, 'I loved the acting, but the plot was confusing,' sentiment analysis can identify your positive feelings about the acting and negative feelings about the plot. Companies often use this to understand how customers feel about their products or services

NLP finds applications in a diverse range of fields, including:

- **Information Retrieval:** Search engines like Google utilize NLP algorithms to deliver relevant search results based on user queries.
- **Machine Translation:** Services like Google Translate employ NLP techniques to translate text between different languages.
- **Text Summarization:** NLP algorithms can condense lengthy documents or articles into concise summaries.

- **Sentiment Analysis:** NLP is used to analyse the sentiment expressed in text data, providing insights into public opinion and customer feedback.
- **Virtual Assistants:** Chatbots and virtual assistants like Siri and Alexa leverage NLP to understand and respond to user queries.

1.4 The Evolution of NLP

The history of NLP spans many years and includes significant changes over time. Initially, it was challenging for researchers to teach computers to understand human language. Language is complex and can be unclear. Early NLP systems used rules created by humans to analyze text. However, these systems struggled with the diverse ways people use language, so they weren't effective for real-world tasks. In the latter half of the 20th century, NLP underwent a major change with the introduction of statistical methods. Researchers started using data-driven approaches and statistical models to study patterns in large amounts of text. Techniques like Hidden Markov Models (HMMs) and Conditional Random Fields (CRFs) allowed NLP

Table 1: Evolution stages of NLP

Evolution Stage	Description	Years	Duration
Early Days	Researchers start working on making computers understand human language. They face challenges due to the complexity of language. Initial systems rely on handcrafted linguistic rules.	1950s-1980s	Around 30 years
Statistical Methods	Researchers begin using statistical methods to analyse text, which improves accuracy by learning patterns from large amounts of data.	1990s	Around 10 years
Rise of Machine Learning	Machine learning techniques become more popular, allowing systems to automatically learn and improve from data without explicit programming.	2000s	Around 10 years
Deep Learning Era	Deep learning, a subset of machine learning, becomes dominant in NLP. Models	2010s	Around 10 years

	like recurrent neural networks (RNNs) and transformers show remarkable performance.		
Current State	NLP continues to evolve rapidly, with ongoing research focusing on areas like contextual understanding, multi-modal interactions, and ethical considerations.	2020s	Ongoing

systems to become more flexible and accurate in tasks such as identifying parts of speech, recognizing named entities, and parsing sentences. Statistical NLP algorithms marked a significant advancement, enabling computers to learn from data and better understand the complexities of natural language.

In the 21st century, deep learning techniques became a game-changer for NLP. Neural networks, especially recurrent and convolutional ones, became powerful tools for working with sequential and structured data, like natural language text. Deep learning models changed how NLP systems understand relationships between words. This led to big improvements in tasks like machine translation, sentiment analysis, and text generation. Word embeddings, like Word2Vec and GloVe, provided dense vector representations of words. These captured the meanings and relationships between words, helping NLP systems achieve top performance on many tasks

In recent years, transformer-based architectures have greatly improved NLP. Models like the Transformer and BERT (Bidirectional Encoder Representations from Transformers) have boosted performance and capabilities. These models use self-attention mechanisms to capture contextual information better. This helps them handle longer texts and understand complex dependencies in language. Transformer-based models have achieved outstanding results in tasks like language modeling, question answering, and document summarization. They set new standards for NLP performance and expand what machines can do in understanding and generating human language.

The evolution of NLP shows the constant drive for innovation and discovery. This progress is thanks to researchers, engineers, and practitioners worldwide. NLP has come a long way, from early rule-based systems to deep learning and transformer architectures. This journey of advancement and growth has been remarkable. It is leading to a future where seamless communication between humans and machines is becoming a reality.

1.5 The Road Ahead

As we start our journey into the world of NLP, we should recognize its vast potential and exciting possibilities. Technology is advancing quickly, and research in NLP is ongoing. NLP keeps evolving, offering new ways to improve communication, automate tasks, and understand the complexities of human language better.

In the following chapters, we will explore the basic concepts, techniques, and applications of NLP in more detail. This will give you the knowledge and skills to understand and work in this dynamic and growing field.

Stay curious, and let's dive into the fascinating world of Natural Language Processing!

------------------- *End of chapter 1* --------------------

2 Fundamental Concepts of Text PreProcessing

In the vast and complex field of NLP, understanding the basic concepts is like building the foundation of a grand structure. These concepts are the building blocks for creating advanced NLP algorithms and models. They help machines understand, analyze, and generate human language. In this chapter, we will explore the main principles of NLP. We will look into the essential techniques and methods that form the backbone of language processing systems.

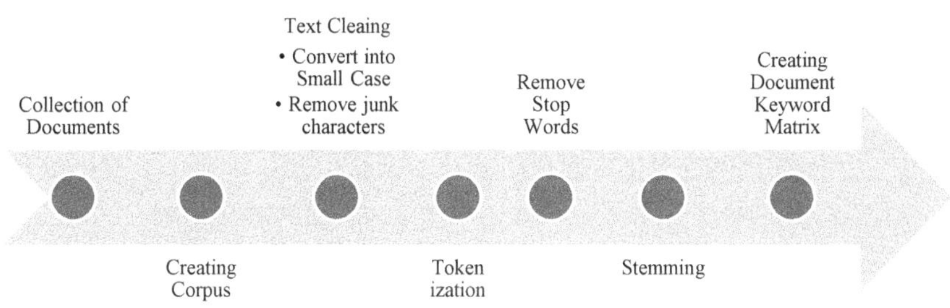

Figure 2:Techniques and methodologies of language processing systems

Text preprocessing is a key part of NLP. It is an important step before any meaningful analysis of text data. Text preprocessing includes tasks like tokenization, stemming, and lemmatization. These tasks transform raw text into a structured and standardized format. By using these techniques, we reduce the complexity of language. This creates a common ground for later NLP tasks, such as sentiment analysis and information extraction.

Parts-of-Speech (POS) tagging is another basic concept in NLP. It is essential for syntactic analysis and understanding language. POS tagging assigns grammatical categories to words in a sentence. This helps machines understand the syntactic structure of text and extract meaningful insights. It identifies nouns, verbs, adjectives, and adverbs. This process is the foundation for more advanced language processing tasks, such as parsing and semantic analysis.

Named Entity Recognition (NER) is a key concept in NLP. It helps machines identify and classify named entities in text. NER can recognize names of people, organizations, and locations. It is important for information extraction, document summarization, and question answering. By identifying entities in text and categorizing them by type, NER helps in understanding and analyzing text better. This opens up many applications in different fields.

In this chapter, we explore these basic concepts in detail. We uncover the techniques and algorithms that are the foundation of NLP systems. By understanding these concepts well, we prepare to explore more advanced NLP tasks and techniques. This sets the stage for a deeper exploration into the intriguing field of language processing.

2.1 What is Text PreProcessing

In the complex world of NLP, data preprocessing is crucial for accurate and effective analysis. This chapter explores data preprocessing in depth, focusing on the essential steps and methods used to transform raw text into a structured format for analysis. Like an artisan refining raw materials into a masterpiece, NLP practitioners carefully prepare text data to extract meaningful insights and unleash the power of language processing systems.

At the beginning of data preprocessing is the vital step of text acquisition. Raw text data comes from various sources like web pages, documents, social media posts, and user-generated content. The quality and entirety of this data are crucial for the next preprocessing steps, highlighting the need for careful data collection practices. Once the text data is gathered, the process of data preprocessing begins. This involves essential steps to clean, structure, and standardize the input data for analysis.

The first step in NLP text preprocessing is converting all letters to lowercase. This standardizes the text data and makes language processing tasks consistent. Converting text to lowercase removes variations in capitalization, simplifies the data, and avoids token duplication caused by case differences. Lowercasing also helps NLP models identify words without being affected by capitalization. This improves the accuracy of tasks like word matching, sentiment analysis, and text classification. Overall, converting text to lowercase is a basic preprocessing step that boosts the efficiency and effectiveness of NLP algorithms by ensuring text data is consistently represented.

Original: "The quick brown fox jumped over the lazy dog. Dogs are wonderful pets!"
Convert to lowercase:
Lowercase: "the quick brown fox jumped over the lazy dog. dogs are wonderful pets!"

The next step is tokenization, where raw text is divided into smaller units or tokens. Tokenization sets the groundwork for further analysis by defining the basic units of text used in language processing tasks. After tokenization, the focus shifts to stop words removal. Common words lacking meaningful semantic value are methodically removed from the text. This process reduces noise and simplifies the data, improving the efficiency and accuracy of subsequent NLP tasks. It enables practitioners to concentrate on the most important aspects of the text.

Original Text: "The quick brown fox jumped over the lazy dog. Dogs are wonderful pets!"
Tokenization (splitting text into individual words or tokens):
Tokens: ["the", "quick", "brown", "fox", "jumped", "over", "the", "lazy", "dog", ".", "dogs", "are", "wonderful", "pets", "!"]

As preprocessing continues, stemming and lemmatization become essential techniques. They normalize words and reduce variations. Stemming removes affixes from words to find their roots. Lemmatization maps words to their base or dictionary forms. These techniques make word representation consistent and help with accurate analysis across the text corpus.

Additionally, the removal of stop words, common words that carry little semantic meaning like "the," "is," and "and," further refines the dataset, eliminating unnecessary information and ensuring the cleanliness and integrity of the input data. Additionally, the removal of junk data, such as HTML tags and punctuation marks, further refines the dataset, eliminating extraneous information and ensuring the cleanliness and integrity of the input data.

Original Text: "The quick brown fox jumped over the lazy dog. Dogs are wonderful pets!"
Stemming or Lemmatization (reducing words to their root form):

Stemmed tokens: ["quick", "brown", "fox", "jump", "lazi", "dog", "dog", "wonder", "pet"]

Removing punctuation and special characters:

Cleaned tokens: ["the", "quick", "brown", "fox", "jumped", "over", "the", "lazy", "dog", "dogs", "are", "wonderful", "pets"]

Removing stop words (commonly occurring words with little semantic meaning):

Tokens after stop word removal: ["quick", "brown", "fox", "jumped", "lazy", "dog", "dogs", "wonderful", "pets"]

Data preprocessing is crucial for NLP to ensure our later analysis is accurate. We begin by collecting the data and then perform tasks like breaking it into tokens, removing stop words, and simplifying words through stemming and lemmatization. We also eliminate any unnecessary junk data. These steps make it easier to understand the text and extract useful information. This chapter explains each step thoroughly, demonstrating how we transform raw text into valuable data for analysis.

2.2 Text Acquisition

Text acquisition is the first step in preprocessing data for NLP tasks. It involves gathering raw text data from sources like web pages, documents, social media, and user-generated content. This step is crucial because the quality and completeness of the dataset affect how well the analysis works later on.

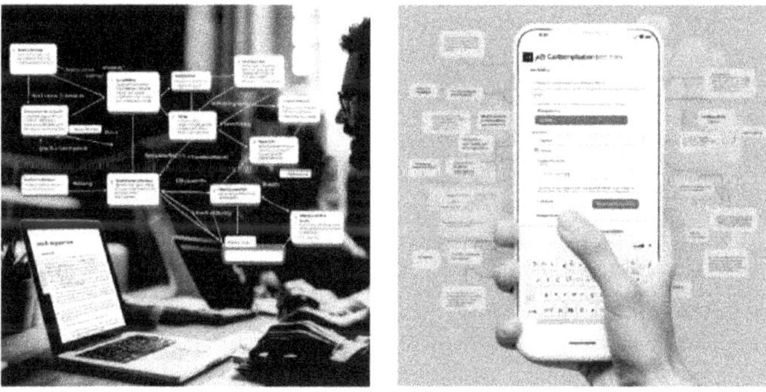

Figure 3: Text acquisition from various sources[1]

There are various methods used for text acquisition, each suitable for different purposes and sources of data. For example, web scraping involves using specialized tools to extract text from web pages automatically. APIs (Application Programming Interfaces) provide a structured way to access text data from online platforms like social media sites, news aggregators, and content repositories. User input allows direct collection of text data from users through forms, surveys, or user-generated content platforms.

Maintaining the integrity and legality of acquired text data is crucial during the acquisition phase. It's important to follow ethical guidelines and data privacy laws, especially with sensitive information or user-generated content. Additionally, data cleaning

---

[1] AI generated image

and validation steps can filter out irrelevant or incorrect data to ensure the dataset is high-quality and reliable.

In conclusion, text acquisition is the first step in the data preprocessing pipeline for NLP. It involves gathering raw text data from various sources while following ethical and legal guidelines. This helps create a strong dataset for meaningful analysis and insights. Good text acquisition practices are crucial for leveraging NLP in different areas like information retrieval, sentiment analysis, machine translation, and text summarization.

2.3 Tokenization

Tokenization is a key step in NLP preprocessing. It breaks text into smaller units called tokens. Tokens are essential for further analysis and tasks in NLP, helping machines understand and work with human language effectively.

At its heart, tokenization divides text into meaningful units, such as words, phrases, or sentences, depending on the task. Word-level tokenization, for instance, separates text into individual words, treating each one as a separate token. This method is often used in tasks like text classification, sentiment analysis, and machine translation, where understanding individual words is important for grasping the text's meaning and context.

Input Paragraph:

"The sun shines brightly in the sky, illuminating the lush green trees below. Birds chirp merrily as they flit from branch to branch, while a playful dog bounds through the grass. The cat lounges lazily on the porch, basking in the warmth of the sun's rays."

Output:

Words:

sun, shines, brightly, sky, illuminating, lush, green, trees, birds, chirp, merrily, flit, branch, playful, dog, bounds, grass, cat, lounges, lazily, porch, basking, warmth, rays.

Phrases:

The sun shines brightly in the sky, illuminating the lush green trees below. Birds chirp merrily as they flit from branch to branch. A playful dog bounds through the grass. The cat lounges lazily on the porch, basking in the warmth of the sun's rays.

Sentence-level tokenization involves dividing text into sentences, treating each sentence as a separate token. This method is valuable in tasks like text summarization, where the aim is to extract essential information from individual sentences. By segmenting text into sentences, machines can better identify and analyze the main ideas and concepts expressed in the text.

Tokenization has challenges. This is especially true for languages without clear word boundaries. It is also true for languages with complex structures. In these cases, special tokenization techniques are needed. These techniques handle the complexities of the language. They ensure the text is accurately segmented. Additionally, tokenization involves other tasks. It may need to handle punctuation marks, special characters, and numbers. The specific task will determine the exact requirements.

In summary, tokenization plays a crucial role in NLP by segmenting text into smaller units for analysis. Whether at the word level or sentence level, tokenization provides the foundation for various language processing tasks, enabling machines to understand, interpret, and generate human language more effectively. By mastering tokenization techniques, practitioners can unlock the full potential of NLP in a wide range of applications and domains.

2.4 Stop Words Removal

Stop words are common words that occur frequently in natural language text but often carry little semantic meaning. Examples of stop words include "the," "and," "is," "in," "to," and "of." In many NLP tasks, stop words can introduce noise and slow down the performance of algorithms by increasing the size of the vocabulary without contributing valuable information. Therefore, a common preprocessing step in NLP is the removal of stop words.

The process of stop words removal involves identifying and eliminating these common words from the text data before analysis.

By filtering out stop words, the focus shifts to the more informative and contextually relevant terms, improving the efficiency and accuracy of downstream NLP tasks. Stop words removal is particularly beneficial in tasks such as document classification, information retrieval, and text summarization, where the emphasis is on identifying important keywords and concepts.

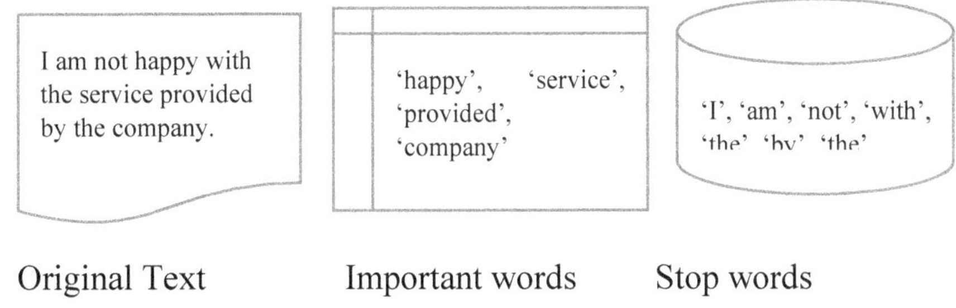

Figure 4: Stop words removal process

However, the determination of which words constitute stop words may vary depending on the specific task, domain, and language. While some words may be universally recognized as stop words across languages, others may carry varying degrees of importance depending on the context. Therefore, stop words lists may need to be customized or adjusted based on the requirements of the analysis and the characteristics of the text data being processed.

One example of the customization of stop words lists based on the requirements of the analysis and the characteristics of the text data being processed can be seen in sentiment analysis tasks.

In sentiment analysis, the goal is to determine the sentiment or emotion expressed in a piece of text. Stop words, which are commonly high-frequency words like "the," "and," "is," etc., are often removed from the text before analysis because they don't carry much sentiment or meaning. However, in certain domains or contexts, some stop words might carry sentiment or contextual importance.

For instance, in a domain like social media, words like "not" or "but" might change the sentiment of a sentence drastically. Consider the sentence "I'm happy, but it's not enough." Here, "not" changes the sentiment from positive to negative. In this case, "not" might be retained in the stop words list to ensure it's not overlooked during sentiment analysis.

So, for sentiment analysis, the stop words list might need changes. This depends on the specific domain and text data. Some words may need to be added or removed from the list.

Despite its advantages, stop words removal is not without its challenges. In certain contexts, stop words may carry essential meaning or serve as distinguishing features of the text. For example, in sentiment analysis, the presence or absence of certain stop words may convey subtle nuances of sentiment or tone. Therefore, careful consideration is required when deciding which stop words to remove and which to retain to ensure that the integrity and meaning of the text are preserved.

In summary, stop words removal is a critical preprocessing step in NLP that aims to improve the efficiency and accuracy of text analysis tasks by filtering out common words that carry little semantic meaning. While it offers significant benefits in terms of noise reduction and focus enhancement, careful consideration is required to balance the removal of stop words with the preservation of important linguistic features and context in the text data.

2.5 Stemming

Stemming is a fundamental text preprocessing technique in NLP that aims to reduce words to their base or root form, known as the stem. The goal of stemming is to normalize variations of words to ensure that different forms of the same word are treated as equivalent. By stripping words of their affixes, such as prefixes and suffixes, stemming helps consolidate vocabulary and improve the efficiency of text analysis tasks.

In this example, the stemmed word "play" can be derived from various original words such as "play "playing," "played," "playful," and "player." This demonstrates how stemming reduces different inflected forms of a word

Table 2: Word Stemming

Original Word	Stemmed
Play	play
Playing	play
Played	play
Playful	play
Player	play

to a common base form, allowing for more efficient text processing and analysis.

One of the most widely used stemming algorithms is the *Porter stemming* algorithm, developed by *Martin Porter* in 1980. The Porter algorithm applies a series of heuristic rules to iteratively remove affixes from words until the stem is reached. While the *Porter* algorithm is simple and computationally efficient, it may produce stems that are not actual words or may result in overstemming, where different words are reduced to the same stem.

Overstemming refers to when the *Porter* algorithm, or any stemming algorithm for that matter, removes too much of a word, leading to two or more distinct words being reduced to the same incorrect stem. Here are some examples:

> **University and Universe:**
> The Porter stemmer might reduce both words to "univers" which wouldn't accurately reflect their different meanings.

Another popular stemming algorithm is the *Snowball stemming* algorithm, also known as the *Porter2 algorithm. Snowball* builds upon the Porter algorithm's principles but introduces additional linguistic rules and refinements to improve accuracy and handle a broader range of linguistic variations. The *Snowball* algorithm is particularly effective for languages other than English and offers better performance in terms of precision and recall.

> Precision and recall are two important metrics used to evaluate the performance of machine learning classification models.

Despite its effectiveness, stemming has some limitations and challenges. One of the main drawbacks is its inability to handle irregular word forms and morphological variations effectively. For example, stemming may produce inaccurate stems for irregular verbs or nouns, leading to potential loss of meaning or ambiguity in the text. Additionally, stemming algorithms may not always account for contextual information or semantic relationships between words, which can impact the accuracy of downstream NLP tasks.

The word "go" and its various morphological variations:

Base form: "go"

Present participle: "going"

Past tense: "went"

Past participle: "gone"

Stemming algorithms might struggle with accurately handling all these variations. However, this oversimplification can lead to loss of meaning or incorrect interpretation, especially in contexts where the tense or aspect of the verb matters.

For example, consider the following sentences:

"She is going to the store."

"He went to the store yesterday."

"The opportunity has gone."

A stemming algorithm that reduces all these forms to "go" might produce:

"She is go to the store."

"He go to the store yesterday."

"The opportunity has go."

In these stemmed versions, the nuances of tense and aspect are lost, resulting in sentences that are grammatically incorrect and semantically confusing. This demonstrates how stemming can struggle to effectively handle irregular word forms and morphological variations, potentially leading to inaccuracies in natural language processing tasks.

In summary, stemming is a valuable text preprocessing technique in NLP that plays a crucial role in normalizing word variations and reducing vocabulary size. While stemming algorithms like *Porter* and *Snowball* offer effective ways to extract word stems, they have limitations in handling irregular word forms and may not always capture semantic nuances. Nonetheless, stemming remains a widely used and indispensable tool for improving the efficiency and accuracy of text analysis tasks in NLP.

2.6 Lemmatization

Lemmatization is a crucial text preprocessing technique in NLP that aims to reduce words to their base or dictionary form, known as the lemma. Unlike stemming, which simply removes affixes to obtain word stems, lemmatization considers the morphological variations of words and maps them to their canonical forms. By normalizing words to their lemmas, lemmatization helps ensure that different inflected forms of the same word are treated as equivalent, thereby improving the accuracy and interpretability of text analysis tasks.

Following table demonstrates how various words are lemmatized to their base or dictionary forms, irrespective of their inflectional or contextual variations.

Table 3: Lemmatization technique

Word	Lemma	Explanation
running	run	The present participle form reduced to its base form.
cats	cat	Plural form reduced to its singular form.
better	good	Comparative form of the adjective "good" is lemmatized.
running	run	Consistency in lemmatization across different contexts.
ate	eat	Past tense form of the verb "eat" is lemmatized.

One of the key advantages of lemmatization over stemming is its ability to produce valid words that are present in the language's dictionary. Instead of blindly applying heuristic rules to strip affixes, lemmatization relies on linguistic knowledge and context to determine the appropriate lemma for each word. For example, the word "ran" would be lemmatized to "run," and "better" would be lemmatized to "good," preserving the semantic integrity of the text.

Lemmatization algorithms use linguistic resources like dictionaries, lexicons, and part-of-speech tags. These resources give information about word forms, meanings, and syntactic categories. This helps algorithms make accurate lemma mappings. Additionally, lemmatization algorithms use context and grammar rules. This helps them handle irregular word forms and morphological variations better.

Despite its advantages, lemmatization may pose challenges, especially when dealing with languages with complex morphological structures or limited linguistic resources. Determining the correct lemma for a word may require analysing its surrounding context and syntactic relationships, which can be computationally expensive and time-consuming. Additionally, lemmatization algorithms may struggle with ambiguous words or homographs, where a single word has multiple possible lemmas depending on its usage and context.

Ambiguity in Context:

Word: "saw"

Context 1: "He saw a saw."

Context 2: "She saw the wood with a saw."

Possible Lemmas:

Context 1: "saw" (noun)

Context 2: "see" (verb)

Explanation: In the first context, "saw" is a noun referring to a cutting tool, while in the second context, it is the past tense form of the verb "see". Lemmatization algorithms may struggle to determine the correct lemma without considering the surrounding context.

Homographs:

Word: "bass"
Context 1: "He caught a big bass."
Context 2: "She played the bass guitar."

Possible Lemmas:
Context 1: "bass" (noun, referring to a fish)
Context 2: "bass" (noun, referring to a musical instrument)

Explanation: "Bass" is a homograph, meaning it has multiple meanings depending on context. Lemmatization algorithms may struggle to disambiguate between these meanings without considering the surrounding linguistic context.

In summary, lemmatization is a valuable text preprocessing technique in NLP that offers advantages over stemming in terms of accuracy and linguistic validity. By mapping words to their canonical forms, lemmatization helps ensure consistency and interpretability in text analysis tasks, ultimately improving the performance of NLP systems. While lemmatization may present challenges in handling complex linguistic structures, its benefits in enhancing the quality and reliability of text processing make it an indispensable tool in NLP.

2.7 Part-of-Speech Tagging

Part-of-Speech (POS) tagging is a fundamental task in NLP that involves assigning grammatical categories or tags to words in a sentence based on their syntactic roles. These categories typically include nouns, verbs, adjectives, adverbs, pronouns, prepositions, conjunctions, and interjections. POS tagging is crucial for understanding the grammatical structure of sentences and extracting meaningful insights from text.

Table 4: Common POS tags

POS Tag	Description
PRP	Personal Pronoun
VBZ	Verb, 3rd person singular present
VBG	Verb, gerund or present participle
TO	to (preposition or infinitive marker)
DT	Determiner
NN	Noun, singular or mass
IN	Preposition or subordinating conjunction
VBD	Verb, past tense
VBP	Verb, non-3rd person singular present
VBN	Verb, past participle

This table provides a comprehensive overview of common POS tags along with their descriptions, helping to understand the roles of different parts of speech in a sentence.

She	is	running	to	the	store
PRP	VBZ	VBG	TO	DT	NN

The	cat	sat	on	the	mat
DT	NN	VBD	IN	DT	NN

I	have	been	studying	all	day
PRP	VBP	VBN	VBG	DT	NN

They	are	playing	football
PRP	VBP	VBG	NN

POS tagging algorithms use different techniques. These techniques include rule-based systems, statistical models, and machine learning algorithms. They use these techniques to assign tags to words in a sentence. Rule-based systems depend on predefined linguistic rules and patterns. They determine the parts of speech of words based on their shape and position in a sentence. Rule-based approaches are simple and easy to understand. However, they may not handle the complexities and subtleties of natural language well.

In contrast, statistical models and machine learning algorithms learn from annotated corpora to probabilistically assign POS tags to words, taking into account contextual information and linguistic features. These models can capture subtle syntactic patterns and linguistic variations, making them more robust and adaptable to different languages and domains. Additionally, machine learning-based POS taggers can leverage features such as word embeddings and syntactic dependencies to improve accuracy and performance.

The applications of POS tagging extend far beyond grammatical analysis, encompassing a wide range of NLP tasks and applications. POS-tagged text serves as input for syntactic parsing, where the grammatical structure of sentences is analysed to identify relationships between words and phrases. POS tagging also plays a crucial role in information extraction, named entity recognition, and sentiment analysis. By accurately labelling words with their parts of speech, NLP systems can disambiguate the meanings of words in context, identify syntactic patterns, and extract valuable insights from textual data.

In summary, part-of-speech tagging is a foundational task in NLP that provides machines with the ability to understand and analyse the grammatical structure of natural language text. Through accurate labelling of words with their respective parts of speech, POS tagging enables machines to extract meaningful insights from text and perform a wide range of language processing tasks. As NLP continues to advance, the importance of POS tagging remains paramount, underscoring its role in enabling machines to navigate and comprehend the complexities of human language.

2.8 Named Entity Recognition

Named Entity Recognition (NER) is a vital NLP task focused on identifying and categorizing named entities within a text. Named entities are specific objects, people, organizations, locations, dates, and other named entities mentioned in the text. NER plays a crucial role in various NLP applications, including information extraction, question answering, document classification, and entity linking. Here are some examples of Names that could be recognized by a NER system:

Table 5: NER Examples

Category	Examples
Person Names	Rahul Sharma, Priya Patel, Amit Singh
Location Names	Mumbai, Delhi, Bangalore
Organization Names	Tata Group, Infosys, Indian Space Research Organisation (ISRO)
Cultural Terms	Diwali, Ganesh Chaturthi, Ramayana
Indian Cuisine	Paneer Tikka, Masala Dosa, Biryani
Historical Figures	Mahatma Gandhi, Rani Lakshmi Bai, Lord Krishna

Indian Cities	Chennai, Kolkata, Uttar Pradesh

NER algorithms utilize a combination of rule-based approaches, statistical models, and machine learning techniques to identify and classify named entities accurately. Rule-based systems rely on predefined patterns and linguistic rules to recognize named entities based on their syntactic and semantic properties. Statistical models and machine learning algorithms, on the other hand, learn from annotated corpora to predict named entity labels based on contextual information and linguistic features.

One of the key challenges in NER is handling ambiguity and variations in named entity mentions. For example, the same entity may be referred to using different aliases, abbreviations, or misspellings throughout the text. NER algorithms must account for these variations and accurately link them to the correct entity in a knowledge base or reference database. Additionally, NER systems must distinguish between named entities and other types of entities or concepts mentioned in the text to avoid false positives.

Suppose we have a text discussing a famous Indian cricketer named "Sachin Tendulkar." Throughout the text, the following variations and ambiguities may arise:

Abbreviation:

"S. Tendulkar"

"Sachin T."

Misspellings:

"Sachin Tendulker"

"Sachin Tendulcar"

Nicknames:

"Master Blaster" (a common nickname for Sachin Tendulkar)

Title or Honorifics:

"Mr. Tendulkar"

"Dr. Sachin"

Initials:

"S. R. Tendulkar"

References without Full Name:

"Tendulkar scored a century yesterday."

NER has numerous practical applications across various domains and industries. In the biomedical domain, NER is used to extract relevant information from scientific literature, such as identifying genes, proteins, diseases, and drug names. In the financial sector, NER helps extract key entities from financial documents, such as company names, stock symbols, and monetary values. In the news and media industry, NER assists in categorizing articles, identifying prominent individuals and organizations, and summarizing news stories based on named entities mentioned.

In summary, NER is a critical NLP task focused on identifying and categorizing named entities within text data. By accurately recognizing and classifying named entities, NER enables machines to extract valuable information, improve information retrieval, and enhance the understanding of textual data across various applications and domains. Despite its challenges, NER continues to play a pivotal role in advancing NLP technologies and facilitating knowledge extraction from unstructured text data.

2.9 Normalization

Normalization is a crucial step in text preprocessing for NLP tasks, aimed at standardizing and harmonizing textual data to improve the efficiency and accuracy of subsequent analyses. This process involves transforming text into a consistent and uniform format, addressing issues such as case sensitivity, punctuation, and numerical representations.

Table 6: Samples of text normalization

Original Text	Normalized Text (Lowercase)	Normalized Text (Uppercase)
The weather in India is quite unpredictable now.	the weather in india is quite unpredictable now.	THE WEATHER IN INDIA IS QUITE UNPREDICTABLE NOW.
I Love to Explore the Beauty of Nature.	i love to explore the beauty of nature.	I LOVE TO EXPLORE THE BEAUTY OF NATURE.
Natural Language Processing is fascinating.	natural language processing is fascinating.	NATURAL LANGUAGE PROCESSING IS FASCINATING.
It's essential to preprocess text data before analysis.	it's essential to preprocess text data before analysis.	IT'S ESSENTIAL TO PREPROCESS TEXT DATA BEFORE ANALYSIS.

One aspect of normalization involves converting text to a consistent case, such as lowercase or uppercase, to ensure uniformity in word representations. By standardizing the case of words, normalization helps avoid duplication and inconsistency in vocabulary, improving the accuracy of text analysis tasks such as document classification and information retrieval.

Another important aspect of normalization is handling punctuation and special characters. These elements can introduce noise and ambiguity in text data, hindering the performance of NLP algorithms. Normalization techniques may involve removing or replacing punctuation marks, converting special characters to their respective ASCII or Unicode representations, or preserving specific punctuation relevant to the context of the analysis.

Original Text: "Hey! How's it going? I'm doing great. 😊 "

Normalized Text: "Hey Hows it going Im doing great"

In this example, the normalization process removed punctuation marks (!, ?, .), converted the special character (😊) to its closest ASCII representation (a smiley face was removed since it doesn't directly translate), and converted all text to lowercase for consistency.

By performing this normalization:

- The text becomes more uniform and easier to process.
- Noise introduced by punctuation and special characters is eliminated.
- NLP algorithms can focus on the content's meaning rather than being distracted by extraneous characters.

It's worth noting that sometimes, specific punctuation marks might be relevant to the context of the analysis (e.g., in sentiment analysis, exclamation marks might indicate strong emotion). In such cases, you might choose to preserve certain punctuation marks or even replace them with specific tokens to retain their meaning in the analysis.

Numeric normalization is also essential in NLP preprocessing, as it involves converting numerical representations into a standardized format. This may include converting numerical values to a common format (e.g., digits or words), handling numerical expressions (e.g., dates, times, currency), and normalizing units of measurement. By standardizing numerical representations, normalization facilitates accurate processing and interpretation of numerical information in text data.

Table 7: Normalization on numerical data

Example	Original Text	Normalized Text
1	"I bought 5 mangoes for rs 100/- each on 15th Mar 2024."	"I bought five mangoes for ₹100 each on 15-03-2024."
2	"The book costs Rs. 450 and was published on 20th June 2023."	"The book costs ₹450 and was published on 20-06-2023."
3	"She received ₹2000 on Sep 5, 2024 as a gift."	"She received ₹2000 on 05-09-2024 as a gift."

In these examples:

- Numerical values, currency amounts, and dates are standardized and normalized according to the Indian format.
- For dates, single-digit days are padded with zeros to maintain a consistent DD-MM-YYYY format.

Overall, normalization plays a crucial role in standardizing textual data and ensuring consistency and uniformity in NLP preprocessing. By addressing issues such as case sensitivity, punctuation, and numerical representations, normalization helps improve the efficiency and accuracy of subsequent text analysis tasks, enabling machines to extract meaningful insights and knowledge from unstructured text data.

2.10 Junk Data Removal

Junk data removal is an essential preprocessing step in NLP that involves the elimination of irrelevant or non-textual elements from the input data. These elements, often referred to as noise, can include HTML tags, URLs, special characters, punctuation marks, and formatting inconsistencies. By cleaning the text data and removing extraneous information, junk data removal helps ensure the integrity and quality of the dataset, improving the effectiveness of subsequent NLP tasks.

One common type of junk data encountered in text data is HTML tags, which are markup elements used to structure web pages. When extracting text from web pages for NLP tasks, it's common to encounter HTML tags that are not relevant to the textual content, such as <div>, <p>, or <span> tags. Junk data removal involves stripping these HTML tags from the text data to extract only the actual textual content, enhancing the accuracy and reliability of subsequent analyses.

<div> <p>This is an example</p> <span>of text with</span> <strong>HTML tags</strong>. </div>	This is an example of text with HTML tags.

Another type of junk data is URLs, which are web addresses embedded within text data. While URLs may provide valuable context or information, they are often irrelevant to the content analysis and can introduce noise in the dataset. Junk data removal techniques may involve replacing URLs with placeholder tokens or entirely removing them from the text data to focus on the textual content itself.

Check out our website at https://www.example.com for more information.	Check out our website at for more information.	Check out our website at [URL] for more information. (Alternatively, the URLs can be replaced with a placeholder token)

Table 8: Junk data removal examples

Original Text	Cleaned Text
<p>Hello, <strong>world!</strong></p>	Hello, world!
Check out our website at https://www.nlp.com	Check out our website at
Hello! How are you? 😊	Hello How are you
The book is interesting!!!	The book is interesting

Special characters, punctuation marks, and formatting inconsistencies are additional sources of noise that can hinder NLP tasks. Junk data removal techniques may include replacing or removing special characters and punctuation marks, standardizing formatting conventions, and handling encoding issues to ensure consistency and uniformity in the text data. By cleaning up these elements, junk data removal improves the readability and analysis of the text, leading to more accurate and reliable results.

In summary, removing junk data is a crucial step in NLP preprocessing. It involves cleaning text data by getting rid of irrelevant or non-text elements. This includes removing noise like HTML tags, URLs, special characters, punctuation marks, and formatting inconsistencies. By removing these elements, we improve the integrity and quality of the dataset. This enhances the effectiveness of later NLP tasks. Careful data cleaning and noise reduction help unlock the full potential of NLP. They allow us to extract meaningful insights and knowledge from unstructured text data.

2.11 Spell Checking and Correction

Spell check and correction is an integral part of NLP text preprocessing, aimed at identifying and rectifying spelling errors in textual data. Spelling mistakes are common in unstructured text data, stemming from typographical errors, keyboard input errors, or linguistic variations. Spell check and correction techniques help improve the accuracy and readability of text data, ensuring that machines can interpret and analyse the content effectively.

One of the primary techniques used in spell check and correction is dictionary-based checking, where words in the text are compared against a predefined dictionary of correctly spelled words. Words not found in the dictionary are flagged as potential spelling errors and are candidates for correction. Additionally, dictionary-based methods may incorporate language-specific rules and patterns to handle common misspellings or variations.

Another way to spell check and correct words uses statistical models and machine learning algorithms. These models are trained on large amounts of text data. The models learn to predict if a word is spelled correctly based on the context and linguistic features around it. By using contextual clues and language patterns, statistical models can find and fix spelling errors with high accuracy. They can even correct words not found in traditional dictionaries.

Spell check and correction techniques may also incorporate morphological analysis and phonetic similarity to improve accuracy. Morphological analysis involves breaking down words into their constituent morphemes and analysing their structural components to identify potential spelling errors. Phonetic similarity measures compare the pronunciation of words to detect and correct phonetically similar words, such as "their" and "there," or "lose" and "loose."

Table 9: Spell checking and correction

Method	Original Text	Corrected Text
Dictionary-based Checking	The bok was intersting.	The book was interesting.
Statistical Models	He is veri good at playin guitar.	He is very good at playing guitar.
Morphological Analysis	She walkes to the park.	She walks to the park.
Phonetic Similarity	Their going to the store.	They're going to the store.

Dictionary-based Checking:

Words like "bok" and "intersting" are flagged as potential spelling errors and corrected using a predefined dictionary.

Statistical Models:

The model identifies contextual cues and linguistic patterns to correct words like "veri" to "very" and "playin" to "playing."

Morphological Analysis:

The structure of the word "walkes" is analysed to correct it to "walks" based on its morphemes.

Phonetic Similarity:

The word "Their" is corrected to "They're" based on phonetic similarity and context.

In summary, spell check and correction are a critical preprocessing step in NLP that addresses spelling errors in textual data. By identifying and rectifying spelling mistakes, spell check and correction techniques enhance the accuracy and readability of text data, enabling machines to interpret and analyze content more effectively. Whether through dictionary-based methods, statistical models, or morphological analysis, spell check and correction play a vital role in ensuring the integrity and quality of text data in NLP applications.

2.12 Noise Reduction

Noise reduction is a crucial aspect of text preprocessing in NLP, aimed at filtering out irrelevant or unwanted elements from textual data to improve the quality and accuracy of subsequent analyses. Noise in text data can arise from various sources, including typographical errors, formatting inconsistencies, duplicate entries, and extraneous information. By eliminating noise, NLP systems can focus on the meaningful content of the text, leading to more reliable and actionable insights.

One common source of noise in text data is typographical errors, which occur due to misspellings, keyboard input errors, or OCR (Optical Character Recognition) inaccuracies. Noise reduction techniques for typographical errors may involve spell check and correction, as discussed earlier, where spelling mistakes are identified and rectified using dictionary-based methods, statistical models, or machine learning algorithms. By fixing typographical errors, noise reduction enhances the readability and interpretability of text data, ensuring that machines can accurately analyse the content.

Formatting inconsistencies are another source of noise in text data, stemming from variations in punctuation, capitalization, and encoding. Noise reduction techniques for formatting inconsistencies may involve normalization, where text is standardized to a consistent format, such as lowercase or uppercase, and special characters and punctuation marks are handled uniformly. By standardizing formatting conventions, noise reduction ensures consistency and uniformity in text data, facilitating accurate analysis and interpretation.

Duplicate entries and extraneous information are additional sources of noise that can hinder NLP tasks. Noise reduction techniques for duplicate entries may involve deduplication, where identical or near-identical entries are identified and removed from the dataset. Similarly, techniques for eliminating extraneous information may involve junk data removal, as discussed earlier, where irrelevant or non-textual elements such as HTML tags, URLs, and special characters are filtered out. By cleaning up duplicate entries and extraneous information, noise reduction enhances the quality and reliability of the text data, leading to more accurate and meaningful analyses.

Original text with noise	The movi was awsm, but the ticket prices at https://www.bookmoive.in are Rs. 500. Also, you can book tickets for the show on 26th April. Don't miss out!
Cleaned text after noise reduction	The movie was awesome, but the ticket prices are Rs. 500. Also, you can book tickets for the show on 26th April. Don't miss out!

In the original text, the following elements can be considered noise:

Typographical errors: "movi" should be "movie" and "awsm" should be "awesome."

URL: https://www.bookmovie.in

Price: Rs. 500

Extraneous information: "you can book tickets for the show on 26th April"

After noise reduction, these irrelevant or unwanted elements are filtered out, leaving only the meaningful content. The cleaned text focuses on the actual review of the movie and removes distractions, improving the quality and accuracy of subsequent analyses in NLP tasks.

In summary, noise reduction is a critical preprocessing step in NLP that involves filtering out irrelevant or unwanted elements from text data to improve the quality and accuracy of subsequent analyses. Whether addressing typographical errors, formatting inconsistencies, duplicate entries, or extraneous information, noise reduction techniques play a vital role in ensuring the integrity and reliability of text data in NLP applications. By eliminating noise, NLP systems can focus on the meaningful content of the text, enabling more effective analysis and interpretation.

2.13 Encoding and Vectorization

Encoding and vectorization are important steps in NLP. They involve changing text data into numerical format. This helps machines process and analyze human language effectively. These steps are crucial for converting raw text into a format that machine learning algorithms can understand. This process makes it possible to perform various NLP tasks. These tasks include text classification, sentiment analysis, and language generation.

2.13.1 One-Hot Encoding

One common encoding technique in NLP is one-hot encoding, where each word in the vocabulary is represented as a binary vector of zeros and ones. In one-hot encoding, a unique index is assigned to each word in the vocabulary, and the corresponding position in the binary vector is set to one to indicate the presence of the word. One-hot encoding creates a sparse and high-dimensional representation of the text data, with each word represented as a unique vector in the vocabulary space.

Example : ["apple", "banana", "cherry", "orange"]

Table 10: One hot encoding

Word	One-Hot Encoded Vector
apple	[1, 0, 0, 0]
banana	[0, 1, 0, 0]
cherry	[0, 0, 1, 0]
orange	[0, 0, 0, 1]

Vocabulary: We have a simple vocabulary containing four words: "apple," "banana," "cherry," and "orange."

One-Hot Encoded Vector: Each word in the vocabulary is represented as a binary vector of zeros and ones.

For example, the word "apple" is represented by the vector [1, 0, 0, 0], where the first position is set to one and the rest are zeros.

Similarly, the word "banana" is represented by the vector [0, 1, 0, 0], indicating the presence of "banana" in the vocabulary.
This way, each word in the vocabulary is uniquely represented by a one-hot encoded vector, creating a sparse and high-dimensional representation of the text data. Each vector has a length equal to the size of the vocabulary, with a single "one" indicating the position of the word in the vocabulary.

2.13.2 Word Embeddings

Another popular encoding technique is word embeddings, which involve representing words as dense, low-dimensional vectors in continuous vector space. Word embeddings capture semantic relationships and contextual information between words, enabling machines to understand the meaning and similarity of words based on their vector representations. Techniques such as Word2Vec, GloVe, and FastText learn word embeddings from large corpora of text data using neural network architectures, capturing syntactic and semantic patterns in word co-occurrence.

Table 11: Word embedding examples

Word	Word2Vec Vector	GloVe Vector	FastText Vector
apple	[0.5, -0.3, 0.8]	[-0.2, 0.4, 0.7]	[0.6, -0.1, 0.9]

banana	[0.4, -0.2, 0.7]	[-0.1, 0.5, 0.6]	[0.5, -0.2, 0.8]
cherry	[0.6, -0.4, 0.9]	[-0.3, 0.6, 0.8]	[0.7, -0.3, 0.9]
orange	[0.3, -0.1, 0.6]	[-0.1, 0.3, 0.5]	[0.4, -0.2, 0.7]

Word: Words from the vocabulary such as "apple," "banana," "cherry," and "orange."

Word2Vec Vector: Vectors representing these words using the Word2Vec embedding technique.

GloVe Vector: Vectors representing these words using the GloVe (Global Vectors for Word Representation) embedding technique.

FastText Vector: Vectors representing these words using the FastText embedding technique.

These are hypothetical vectors for illustration purposes. In practice, word embeddings capture semantic relationships and contextual information between words in a dense, low-dimensional vector space, allowing machines to understand the meaning and similarity of words based on their vector representations.

2.13.3 Vectorization with TF-IDF

Vectorization in NLP extends beyond individual words to encompass entire documents or text sequences. Document vectorization techniques such as TF-IDF (Term Frequency-Inverse

Document Frequency) represent documents as vectors based on the frequency of words and their importance in the document corpus. TF-IDF assigns higher weights to words that are frequent in a document but rare in the overall corpus, capturing the discriminative power of words in representing document content.

Corpus:

Consider a corpus containing three documents:

1. Document 1: "apple banana apple"
2. Document 2: "banana cherry orange"
3. Document 3: "apple cherry cherry"

Using TF-IDF, we can compute the vector representations for these documents:

Table 12: Vectorization with TFIDF

Term	Document 1	Document 2	Document 3
apple	2	0	1
banana	1	1	0
cherry	0	1	2
orange	0	1	0

TF-IDF Calculation

For example, let's calculate the TF-IDF score for the term "apple" in Document 1:

TF (Term Frequency):

Number of times "apple" appears in Document 1 = 2

IDF (Inverse Document Frequency):

Total number of documents = 3

Number of documents containing "apple" = 2

IDF = log(3 / 2) ≈ 0.176

TF-IDF Score:

TF-IDF = TF * IDF = 2 * 0.176 = 0.352

TF-IDF Vectorized Representation

The TF-IDF vector for Document 1 would be [0.352, 0, 0, 0], and similarly, vectors can be computed for the other documents based on their term frequencies and IDF scores.

Term: Words from the corpus, such as "apple," "banana," "cherry," and "orange."

TF (Term Frequency): The frequency of each term in the respective documents.

IDF (Inverse Document Frequency): The logarithmically scaled inverse fraction of the documents that contain the term, providing a measure of the term's importance.

TF-IDF Vectorized Representation: The final vector representation for each document based on the computed TF-IDF scores.

TF-IDF vectorization captures the importance of words in individual documents relative to the entire corpus, providing a rich representation that highlights the discriminative power of words in capturing document content.

Table 13: Encoding vs. Vectorization

Aspect	Encoding	Vectorization
Purpose	Convert textual data to numerical format	Transform text data into vectors of numerical values
Granularity	Lower-level (individual words or characters)	Higher-level (words, phrases, or entire documents)
Representation	Sparse (e.g., one-hot encoding)	Dense (e.g., word embeddings, TF-IDF vectors)
Semantic Capture	Limited, mainly positional or categorical information	Rich, captures semantic relationships and contextual information
Complexity	Simpler and more straightforward	More complex, capturing nuanced semantic meanings

Examples	- One-Hot Encoding - Label Encoding	- Word Embeddings (Word2Vec, GloVe, FastText) - TF-IDF

In summary, encoding and vectorization are important steps in NLP. They help machines understand and process human language effectively. These processes convert text data into numerical representations. Examples include one-hot encoding, word embeddings, and document vectors. Encoding and vectorization make it easier to perform various NLP tasks.

They also help develop advanced language processing models. These techniques are crucial for improving NLP systems. They unlock the potential of text data for analysis and interpretation.

------------------- *End of chapter 2* -------------------

3 Statistical Methods in NLP

Statistical methods are the foundation of many NLP techniques. They offer powerful tools for analyzing, modeling, and understanding human language. In this chapter, we explore the basic principles of statistical methods in NLP. We also look at how they are used to solve various language-related problems. These methods include probabilistic models and distributional semantics. Statistical approaches provide a strong framework for extracting insights from text data. They also help in building advanced language processing systems.

At the heart of statistical methods in NLP is the idea of modeling language as a probabilistic phenomenon. This means treating language as a random process. Statistical models capture the uncertainty and variability in human communication. They use statistical techniques like probability theory, statistical inference, and machine learning algorithms. These models analyze linguistic patterns, predict linguistic phenomena, and generate coherent text. They are used in tasks like language modeling and sequence labeling. Statistical methods offer versatile tools for various NLP tasks. They help tackle real-world language challenges effectively.

In this chapter, we will explore key statistical methods and techniques used in NLP, including n-gram models, Hidden Markov

Models (HMMs), Conditional Random Fields (CRFs), and more. We will examine how these methods are applied in various NLP applications, such as part-of-speech tagging, named entity recognition, sentiment analysis, and machine translation.

3.1 Introduction to probability and statistics in NLP

In Natural Language Processing, probability and statistics play a key role. They help us make sense of language data and deal with uncertainties in language. This section will introduce you to the basic concepts of probability and statistics in NLP and explain why they are important.

3.1.1 Probability in NLP

Probability theory helps us understand how likely different language events are to happen. It gives us tools to deal with uncertainty in language and make predictions based on data. We'll cover basic ideas like *probability distributions* and more advanced topics like *Bayesian inference*, which help us model and predict language patterns.

Example:

Imagine you have a sentence: "The cat sits on the mat." Probability theory helps us understand how likely it is to see a word like "cat" following the word "The" in English sentences. By analyzing many sentences, we can estimate the probability of different words appearing together, helping us predict the next word in a sentence or understand the structure of language better.

3.1.2 Statistics in NLP

Statistics is all about analyzing data to find useful information and patterns. In NLP, we use statistical methods to learn from language data, estimate model settings, and understand language properties. Techniques like hypothesis testing, regression analysis, and machine learning help us uncover relationships, categorize text, and create models for different NLP tasks.

Example:
Suppose we have a dataset of movie reviews. We can use statistical methods to analyze the reviews and find out which words or phrases are commonly used in positive reviews compared to negative ones. Techniques like machine learning can help us classify reviews as positive or negative based on these patterns, improving sentiment analysis in NLP.

Combining probability and statistics helps us understand language structures, meanings, and usage patterns. This understanding is vital for building accurate and reliable language processing systems that can perform tasks like translation, sentiment analysis, and information extraction effectively.

In the upcoming sections, we'll dive deeper into specific probabilistic models and statistical methods used in NLP. We'll discuss how these models and methods work, their applications, and how they contribute to our understanding and processing of natural language data.

3.1.2.1 N-grams and language models

N-grams are a fundamental concept in NLP, representing contiguous sequences of N tokens (or words) in a text document. These sequences capture the local context and dependencies between adjacent words, providing valuable insights into the structure and patterns of language. N-grams serve as the building blocks for constructing language models, which are statistical models that estimate the probability of word sequences occurring in a given text corpus.

Language models based on N-grams are widely used in NLP for tasks such as text generation, spell checking, and speech recognition. These models leverage the frequency of N-gram occurrences in a training corpus to estimate the probability of observing a particular word given its context.

For example, a bigram model estimates the probability of a word based on the preceding word, while a trigram model considers the probabilities of word sequences of length three.

3.1.2.1.1 Bigram Model

In a bigram model, the probability of a word is estimated based on the preceding word. It assumes that each word in a sentence depends only on its immediate predecessor.

Example:

Consider the sentence: "I love ice cream."

Here, we look at pairs of consecutive words (bigrams):

"I love"

"love ice"

"ice cream"

The bigram model estimates the probability of the second word based on the first word in each pair.

For instance, it calculates:

- P ("love"|"I")
- P ("ice"|"love")

These probabilities are estimated from a corpus of text data by counting how often each bigram appears relative to its preceding word.

3.1.2.1.2 Trigram Model

In a trigram model, the probability of a word is estimated based on the two preceding words. It considers sequences of three words to predict the next word.

Example:

Using the same sentence, "I love ice cream":

Here, we look at sequences of three consecutive words (trigrams):

"I love ice"

"love ice cream"

The trigram model estimates the probability of the third word based on the first two words in each sequence.

For example, it calculates:

P ("ice"|"I love")

P ("cream"|"love ice")

Similarly, these probabilities are estimated from a corpus by counting the occurrences of each trigram relative to its two preceding words.

Both models help in understanding the structure and patterns in language by quantifying the likelihood of word sequences, which is essential for tasks like text prediction, machine translation, and more.

One of the key advantages of N-grams and language models is their simplicity and efficiency in capturing local linguistic dependencies. By focusing on short sequences of words, N-gram models can approximate the underlying structure of language and generate coherent text with relatively low computational overhead. However, N-gram models may struggle with long-range dependencies and suffer from data sparsity issues when encountering unseen word sequences.

Long-Range Dependencies

Consider the following sentences:

"The cat sat on the mat."

"The dog barked loudly outside."

In these sentences, the word "cat" is followed by "sat," and the word "dog" is followed by "barked." If we use a bigram model to predict the next word based on the preceding word, it might struggle with long-range dependencies.

Bigram Model Predictions

P ("sat"|"cat") might be high based on the first sentence.

P ("barked"|"dog") might also be high based on the second sentence.

However, if we want to predict the word following "cat" based on the context provided by "dog," the bigram model will not capture this long-range dependency effectively.

Data Sparsity Issues

Imagine we have a corpus where the sentence "I love ice cream" appears frequently, but the sentence "I love chocolate ice cream" is rare or even absent.

Trigram Model Predictions

P ("cream"|"chocolate ice") would be difficult to estimate accurately because of the lack of occurrences of this trigram in the training data. Due to data sparsity, the model might assign a low probability to the trigram "chocolate ice cream," even though it makes perfect sense in the context.

Long-Range Dependencies: N-gram models might struggle to capture relationships between words that are separated by several other words, as they only consider local contexts.

Data Sparsity: When encountering unseen or rare word sequences, the model may not have enough data to estimate accurate probabilities, leading to less reliable predictions.

Despite their limitations, N-grams and language models remain widely used in NLP due to their effectiveness and versatility. From predictive typing on smartphones to machine translation systems, N-gram models power a wide range of language processing applications, providing valuable insights into the statistical properties of natural language and enabling machines to generate human-like text with remarkable accuracy.

3.2 TF-IDF

TF-IDF (Term Frequency-Inverse Document Frequency) is a statistical measure used to evaluate the importance of a term within a collection of documents or corpus. It is a widely used technique in NLP for text mining, information retrieval, and document classification tasks. TF-IDF aims to highlight terms that are both frequent within individual documents and rare across the entire corpus, thereby emphasizing their significance in characterizing the content of documents.

Note for Readers:

You may notice that the concept of TF-IDF (Term Frequency-Inverse Document Frequency) is discussed in chapter 2 and also in this chapter. This repetition aims to provide a comprehensive understanding from different perspectives: its role in encoding and vectorization, and its statistical foundations and applications. We encourage you to refer to both discussions to gain a holistic view of TF-IDF's significance in natural language processing.

The TF (Term Frequency) component of TF-IDF measures the frequency of a term within a document. It represents how often a term occurs in a document relative to the total number of terms in that document. Terms that appear frequently within a document are assumed to be more relevant to the document's content and are assigned higher TF values.

The IDF (Inverse Document Frequency) component of TF-IDF measures the rarity of a term across the entire corpus. It evaluates how much information a term provides by considering its distribution across all documents in the corpus. Terms that appear in many documents are considered less informative and are assigned lower IDF values, while terms that appear in fewer documents are deemed more valuable and are assigned higher IDF values.

The TF-IDF score for a term in a document is computed by multiplying its TF value by its IDF value. This results in a numerical representation of the term's importance within the document relative to the entire corpus. Terms with high TF-IDF scores are considered significant to the document's content and are often used as features in text analysis tasks such as keyword extraction, document ranking, and content recommendation.

Let's understand how to calculate TF-IDF.

TF-IDF Calculation Steps:

- **Tokenization:** Break down the text into individual words or tokens.
- **Term Frequency (TF):** Calculate the frequency of each word in the document.
- **Document Frequency (DF):** Calculate the number of documents that contain each word.

- **Inverse Document Frequency (IDF):** Calculate the IDF value for each word.
- **TF-IDF Calculation:** Multiply TF by IDF to get the TF-IDF score for each word in the document.

Example Document Set:

Let's consider a small set of documents related to different fruits:

Document 1: "apple banana apple"

Document 2: "banana cherry orange"

Document 3: "apple cherry cherry"

Step 1: Tokenization

Tokenize each document into individual words:

Document 1: ["apple", "banana", "apple"]

Document 2: ["banana", "cherry", "orange"]

Document 3: ["apple", "cherry", "cherry"]

Step 2: Term Frequency (TF)

Calculate the frequency of each word in each document:

Document 1:

apple: 2

banana: 1

Document 2:

banana: 1

cherry: 1

orange: 1

Document 3:

apple: 1

cherry: 2

Step 3: Document Frequency (DF)

Calculate the number of documents that contain each word:

apple: 3

banana: 2

cherry: 2

orange: 1

Step 4: Inverse Document Frequency (IDF)

Calculate the IDF value for each word using the formula:

$$\mathrm{IDF}(w) = \log\left(\frac{\text{Total number of documents}}{\text{Number of documents containing } w}\right)$$

For example:

- IDF(apple) = log(3/3) = log(1) = 0
- IDF(banana) = log(3/2) = log(1.5) ≈ 0.176
- IDF(cherry) = log(3/2) = log(1.5) ≈ 0.176
- IDF(orange) = log(3/1) = log(3) ≈ 0.477

Step 5: TF-IDF Calculation

Multiply the TF value of each word by its IDF value:

Document 1:

apple: 2 * 0 = 0

banana: 1 * 0.176 ≈ 0.176

Document 2:

banana: 1 * 0.176 ≈ 0.176

cherry: 1 * 0.176 ≈ 0.176

orange: 1 * 0.477 ≈ 0.477

Document 3:

apple: 1 * 0 = 0

cherry: 2 * 0.176 ≈ 0.352

TF-IDF Vectorized Representation

Combine the TF-IDF scores to represent each document as a vector:

Document 1: [0, 0.176, 0]

Document 2: [0, 0.176, 0.176, 0.477]

Document 3: [0, 0, 0.352]

TF-IDF captures the importance of words in documents by weighing the term frequency (TF) against the inverse document frequency (IDF). In this example, words like "orange" and "cherry" that are less frequent across the corpus but specific to certain documents have higher TF-IDF scores, indicating their importance in those documents. On the other hand, common words like "apple" and "banana" have lower TF-IDF scores, reflecting their lower discriminative power.

3.3 Advanced Word Embedding Techniques

Word embeddings transform words into continuous vector representations, capturing semantic relationships and context.

3.3.1 Word2Vec

Word2Vec (W2V) is a groundbreaking technique in the field of NLP that revolutionized the way we represent and understand words in textual data. Developed by a team of researchers at Google led by *Tomas Mikolov*. Word2Vec enables the creation of dense, low-dimensional vector representations of words based on their contextual usage in a large corpus of text. This approach captures semantic relationships between words by mapping them to points in a continuous vector space, where similar words are located closer together. The underlying idea behind Word2Vec is that words with similar meanings tend to occur in similar contexts and therefore should have similar vector representations.

There are two main architectures for training Word2Vec models: Continuous Bag of Words (CBOW) and Skip-gram. In the CBOW architecture, the model predicts the target word based on its surrounding context words, while in the Skip-gram architecture, the model predicts the context words based on the target word.

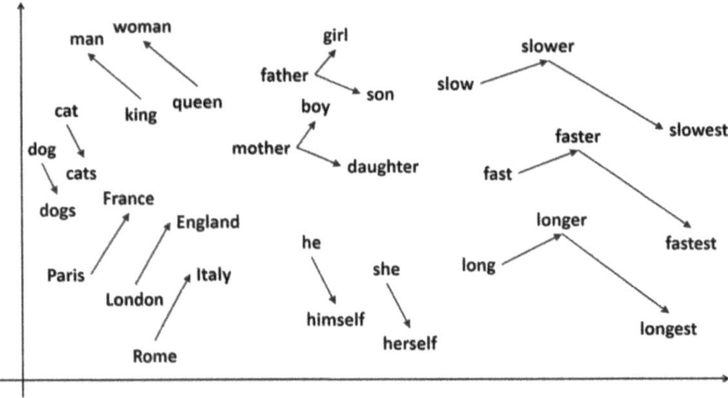

Figure 5: Word2Vec Representation[2]

Both architectures learn to predict the occurrence of words based on their context, effectively capturing the distributional semantics of words in the text. Once trained, the Word2Vec model produces dense, fixed-length vectors for each word in the vocabulary, which can then be used as feature representations in various NLP tasks.

Word2Vec has found widespread applications in NLP tasks such as sentiment analysis, document classification, machine translation, and word similarity calculation. By representing words as vectors in a continuous vector space, Word2Vec captures subtle semantic relationships between words and enables machines to understand and process language more effectively.

---

[2] Image source : https://samyzaf.com/ML/nlp/word2vec2.png

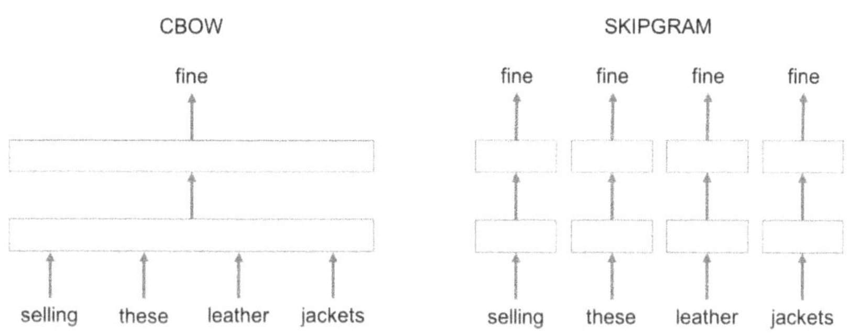

Figure 6: CBOW vs. SKIPGRAM[3]

Moreover, the dense vector representations learned by Word2Vec models are computationally efficient and can be easily incorporated into neural network architectures for further learning and processing tasks. Overall, Word2Vec has become an indispensable tool in the NLP toolkit, empowering researchers and practitioners to develop more sophisticated language processing systems with improved performance and efficiency.

3.3.2 GloVe

GloVe, short for Global Vectors for Word Representation, is a popular word embedding technique. It aims to understand how words relate in a large collection of text. Researchers at Stanford

[3] Image source : https://fasttext.cc/img/cbo_vs_skipgram.png

University developed GloVe. It learns how words are represented by studying how often they appear together in the text. GloVe uses an objective function to optimize word relationships based on their co-occurrence probabilities. This function helps GloVe capture the importance of word pairs. Unlike Word2Vec, which looks at nearby words, GloVe examines the entire text collection. This method helps GloVe understand both the structure and meaning of words in sentences.

The key idea behind GloVe is that the ratio of co-occurrence probabilities between word pairs encodes valuable information about the semantic relationships between words. By optimizing an objective function based on these ratios, GloVe learns dense vector representations for words in a continuous vector space, where similar words are located closer together. This approach enables GloVe to capture global word-word relationships and produce high-quality word embeddings that preserve semantic similarities and capture linguistic regularities.

The first step in GloVe is to construct a co-occurrence matrix from the corpus. The matrix X has dimensions $V \times V$, where V is the vocabulary size. Each entry Xij in the matrix represents the number of times word j appears in the context of word i.

Objective Function

The core of GloVe is its objective function, which aims to learn word vectors that preserve the ratios of co-occurrence probabilities between words. The objective function is defined as:

$$J = \sum_{i,j=1}^{V} f(X_{ij})(w_i^T \tilde{w}_j + b_i + \tilde{b}_j - \log(X_{ij}))^2$$

Where:

- Xij is the co-occurrence count between word i and word j.
- wi and $w'j$ are the word vectors for word i and word j, respectively.
- bi and $b'j$ are the biases for word i and word j, respectively.
- f is a weighting function used to mitigate the effect of very frequent co-occurrences.
- A common choice is,

$$f(x) = \min\left(1, (\frac{x}{x_{\max}})^{\alpha}\right)$$

The goal of optimizing this objective function is to minimize the difference between the dot product of word vectors and biases and the logarithm of their co-occurrence counts, weighted by f.

Imagine we have a small corpus consisting of the following sentences:

1) "I love ice cream."
2) "I love chocolate."
3) "Ice cream is delicious."
4) "Chocolate is sweet."

From this corpus, we can construct a word-word co-occurrence matrix. For simplicity, let's consider a window size of one word to the left and one word to the right of the target word.

The co-occurrence counts might look something like this:

	I	love	ice	cream	chocolate	is	delicious	sweet
I	0	2	1	1	1	1	0	0
love	2	0	1	1	1	0	0	0
ice	1	1	0	2	0	1	0	0
cream	1	1	2	0	0	1	1	0
chocolate	1	1	0	0	0	1	0	1
is	1	0	1	1	1	0	1	1

delicious	0	0	0	1	0	1	0	1
sweet	0	0	0	0	1	1	1	0

In this matrix:

- The rows represent the target words.
- The columns represent the context words.
- Each cell Xij contains the co-occurrence count between the target word (row) and the context word (column).

This co-occurrence matrix serves as the input for training the GloVe model, where the model learns to produce word vectors that capture the semantic relationships between words based on their co-occurrence statistics in the corpus.

Syntactic information refers to the grammatical structure and arrangement of words in sentences. It deals with the relationships between words that are defined by the grammar of a language, such as subject-verb, adjective-noun, or preposition-object relationships.

In the context of GloVe:

Examples: Word order, grammatical roles, and syntactic dependencies.

Role in GloVe: Syntactic information helps the model understand the structural aspects of language, such as how words relate to each other within sentences.

GloVe can capture syntactic patterns by observing which words frequently appear together in specific grammatical roles or structures. For example, "I love" might frequently co-occur with "ice cream" or "chocolate," indicating syntactic relationships like subject-verb-object.

Semantic information refers to the meaning of words and how words relate to real-world concepts. It deals with the interpretation and understanding of the content conveyed by words, phrases, or sentences.

In the context of GloVe:

Examples: Word meanings, synonyms, antonyms, and semantic relationships between words.

Role in GloVe: Semantic information helps the model capture the deeper meaning of words and their relationships based on the context in which they appear.

GloVe captures semantic relationships by observing which words tend to appear in similar contexts or convey similar meanings. Words like "ice cream" and "chocolate" might frequently co-occur in dessert-related contexts, indicating a semantic relationship based on shared meaning.

GloVe has been widely adopted in various NLP tasks, including sentiment analysis, machine translation, and document clustering. Its ability to capture both syntactic and semantic information makes it particularly effective for tasks that require understanding the nuanced relationships between words. Moreover, GloVe embeddings are computationally efficient and easy to use, making them suitable for large-scale NLP applications. Overall, GloVe has become an indispensable tool in the NLP toolkit, offering researchers and practitioners a powerful method for representing and understanding the meaning of words in textual data.

3.3.3 FastText

FastText is an extension of the popular Word2Vec model developed by Facebook AI Research. Unlike Word2Vec, which generates embeddings at the word level, FastText operates at the subword level, allowing it to capture morphological information and handle out-of-vocabulary words more effectively. The key innovation of FastText lies in its use of character n-grams, which are sequences of characters of length n, as the basic units of representation. By representing words as a bag of character n-grams, FastText is able to capture the internal structure and morphology of words, enabling it to generate embeddings for unseen words and rare words more accurately.

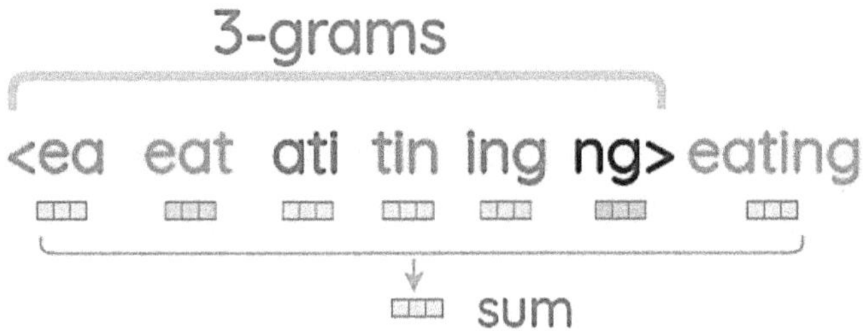

Figure 7: FastText center word embedding[4]

One of the main advantages of FastText is its ability to handle morphologically rich languages and out-of-vocabulary words, which are common challenges in many NLP tasks. By leveraging character n-grams, FastText is able to generalize well to unseen words by composing embeddings from their constituent character n-grams. This makes FastText particularly effective for tasks such as sentiment analysis, text classification, and machine translation, where the vocabulary may be diverse and dynamic.

Lets understand the example given in an image,

---

[4] Image source : https://amitness.com/posts/images/fasttext-center-word-embedding.png

Word: "eating"

Character Trigrams (3-grams) - A trigram is a sequence of three characters.

For the word "eating", the character trigrams are:

1) "eat"
2) "ati"
3) "tin"
4) "ing"

FastText computes embeddings for words by averaging the embeddings of their constituent character n-grams. For the purpose of this example, let's assume we have pre-trained embeddings for each character trigram.

Hypothetical Character Trigram Embeddings:

Let's say the embeddings for the character trigrams "eat", "ati", "tin", and "ing" are as follows (these are hypothetical embeddings for illustration purposes):

1) "eat": [0.2, -0.3, 0.5]
2) "ati": [-0.1, 0.4, -0.2]
3) "tin": [0.3, 0.1, -0.4]
4) "ing": [-0.2, 0.5, 0.3]

To compute the FastText embedding for "eating", we average the embeddings of its constituent character trigrams:

$$\text{Embedding}(\text{"eating"}) = \frac{\text{Embedding}(\text{"eat"})+\text{Embedding}(\text{"ati"})+\text{Embedding}(\text{"tin"})+\text{Embedding}(\text{"ing"})}{4}$$

Substituting the hypothetical embeddings:

$$\text{Embedding}(\text{"eating"}) = \frac{[0.2,-0.3,0.5]+[-0.1,0.4,-0.2]+[0.3,0.1,-0.4]+[-0.2,0.5,0.3]}{4}$$

$$\text{Embedding}(\text{"eating"}) = \frac{[0.2-0.1+0.3-0.2,-0.3+0.4+0.1+0.5,0.5-0.2-0.4+0.3]}{4}$$

$$\text{Embedding}(\text{"eating"}) = \frac{[0.2,0.7,0.2]}{4}$$

$$\text{Embedding}(\text{"eating"}) = [0.05, 0.175, 0.05]$$

So, the FastText embedding for the word "eating" would be approximately [0.05, 0.175, 0.05].

This example illustrates how FastText leverages character trigrams to compute embeddings for words, enabling it to handle morphologically rich languages and out-of-vocabulary words effectively.

In addition to its robustness to out-of-vocabulary words, FastText is also computationally efficient and scalable, making it suitable for large-scale NLP applications. The model can be trained on large corpora of text data using techniques like hierarchical s*oftmax* and *negative sampling*, allowing it to generate high-quality embeddings efficiently. Overall, FastText has become a popular choice for word representation in NLP, offering a powerful and versatile tool for capturing the meaning and structure of words in textual data.

3.3.4 BERT

BERT, which stands for Bidirectional Encoder Representations from Transformers, is a revolutionary language model introduced by Google Research in 2018. BERT adopts a bidirectional approach, allowing it to capture contextual information from both directions within a text sequence. This bidirectional understanding enables BERT to generate more accurate and contextually rich representations of words, phrases, and sentences, leading to significant improvements in various NLP tasks.

At the heart of BERT lies the transformer architecture, which has gained widespread popularity in recent years for its ability to model long-range dependencies and capture complex relationships in sequential data. BERT employs a multi-layer bidirectional transformer encoder, which processes input sequences using self-attention mechanisms to compute contextualized representations of each token. By leveraging self-attention, BERT is able to capture dependencies between words that are far apart in the input sequence, allowing it to generate more informative embeddings.

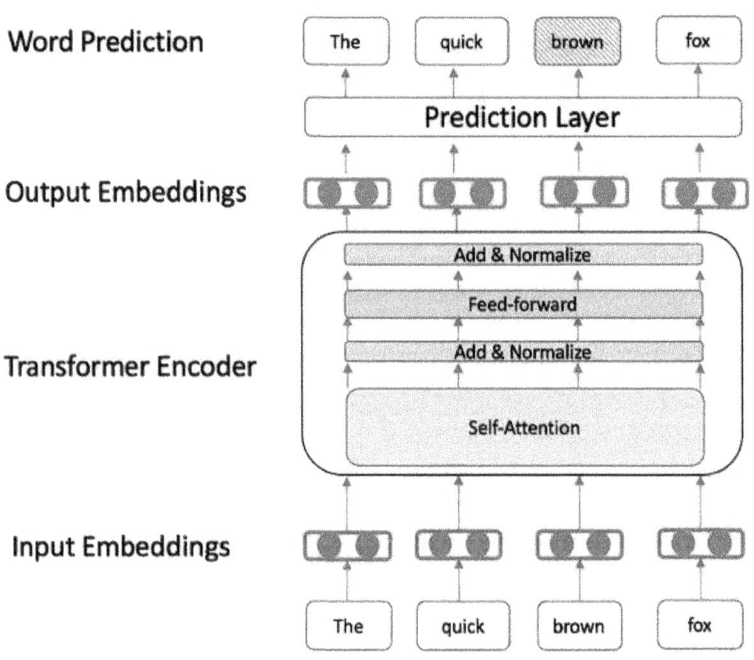

Figure 8: BERT Model[5]

Example

Consider the sentence: "I went to the bank to deposit some money." In this sentence, the word "bank" can have different meanings based on the context:

1. "bank" as a financial institution

[5] Image source : https://www.researchgate.net/profile/Simon_Baker11/publication/347822270/figure/fig5/AS:972409607823368@1608851925584/An-illustration-of-the-BERT-model-The-model-is-predicting-the-masked-word-brown_W640.jpg

2. "bank" as the side of a river

Traditional models might struggle to determine the correct meaning of "bank" without considering the surrounding context.

Now, let's see how BERT processes this sentence:

1. **Tokenization:** BERT first tokenizes the input sentence into individual tokens:
   ["I", "went", "to", "the", "bank", "to", "deposit", "some", "money", "."]
2. **Embedding:** Each token is then converted into an embedding vector.
3. **Self-Attention Mechanism:** BERT's transformer layers use self-attention to weigh the importance of each token in the context of the whole sentence. This allows BERT to capture dependencies between words, even if they are far apart in the input sequence.
4. **Contextual Representation:** After passing through multiple transformer layers, each token's representation is refined to capture its contextual meaning in the sentence.

For this example, the contextual representation of the word "bank" would consider its surrounding tokens like "to the" and "to deposit some money", helping BERT determine its correct meaning based on the context.

In this example, BERT's bidirectional approach and transformer architecture enable it to understand the context and correctly interpret the ambiguous word "bank", showcasing its capability to handle complex language tasks effectively.

One of the key innovations of BERT is its pretraining approach, which involves training the model on large amounts of unlabeled text data using two unsupervised tasks: *masked language modeling* and *next sentence prediction*. During pretraining, BERT learns to predict masked-out tokens within a sequence and to determine whether two input sentences are contiguous or not. This pretraining enables BERT to acquire a deep understanding of the syntactic and semantic structures of language, making it a powerful tool for a wide range of downstream NLP tasks, including text classification, named entity recognition, question answering, and sentiment analysis. Overall, BERT has revolutionized the field of NLP, setting new benchmarks and pushing the boundaries of what is possible in language understanding and generation tasks.

- **Masked Language Modeling**

  In this task, BERT learns to predict masked-out tokens within a sequence.

  Example:

  Input Sentence: "The cat [MASK] on the [MASK]."

BERT tries to predict the masked words based on the context:
Predicted Tokens: "sat", "mat"
Here, BERT learns the context "The cat" and predicts the missing words "sat" and "mat" based on its understanding of language structures.

- **Next Sentence Prediction**
  In this task, BERT learns to determine whether two input sentences are contiguous or not.
  Example:
  Input Pair: "I love reading books." [SEP] "Books are great."
  BERT learns to predict whether the second sentence follows the first one. Predicted Label: "IsNext"
  BERT uses this training to understand the relationships between sentences and the continuity of ideas, which is crucial for tasks like question answering and text summarization.

Impact on Downstream Tasks

After pretraining on these tasks, BERT's learned representations capture rich semantic and syntactic information, which makes it highly effective for various downstream NLP tasks.

Examples:

- **Text Classification:**

  Given a sentence, BERT can classify it into predefined categories like sentiment analysis (positive/negative) or topic classification (politics, sports, technology, movies).

  Input: "Scientists have discovered a new species of marine life deep in the Pacific Ocean!"

  Output: Science

- **Named Entity Recognition (NER):**

  BERT can identify and classify named entities like names, organizations, and dates in text.

  Input: "Apple announced a new product called iPhone 13."

  Output:

  Entity: Apple (Organization)

  Entity: iPhone 13 (Product)

- **Question Answering:**

  BERT can answer questions based on a given context.

  Context: "BERT is a powerful NLP model introduced by Google."

  Question: "Who introduced BERT?"

  Answer: Google

- **Sentiment Analysis:**

  BERT can determine the sentiment expressed in a sentence.

Input: "I had a terrible day at work."

Output: Negative Sentiment

BERT has introduced a new era in natural language processing with its innovative pretraining approach and transformer architecture. It learns language intricacies through tasks like masked language modeling and next sentence prediction, setting new standards across many NLP tasks. BERT understands context well, captures both grammar and meaning subtleties, and generates accurate and context-rich representations. Its capabilities have significantly changed how we understand and generate language, marking a pivotal advancement in NLP. As we explore further possibilities in NLP, BERT showcases the impact of deep learning and pretraining in shaping the future of intelligent language processing.

3.3.5 GPT

Generative Pretrained Transformer (GPT) is a cutting-edge language model developed by OpenAI that has garnered significant attention in the field of NLP. GPT belongs to the family of transformer-based models and is renowned for its ability to generate coherent and contextually relevant text. Unlike traditional language models that generate text sequentially, GPT utilizes a transformer decoder architecture with self-attention mechanisms, allowing it to capture long-range dependencies and generate text word by word in a highly parallelized manner.

One of the distinguishing features of GPT is its pretraining approach, which involves training the model on vast amounts of text data using unsupervised learning tasks. GPT is trained to predict the next word in a sequence given the preceding context, a task known as autoregressive language modeling. This pretraining process enables GPT to learn rich representations of language and develop an understanding of syntactic and semantic structures, making it capable of generating coherent and contextually appropriate text across a wide range of topics and styles.

GPT has demonstrated impressive performance on various NLP tasks, including text completion, summarization, translation, and dialogue generation. Its ability to generate human-like text has led to its adoption in applications such as content generation, chatbots, and language understanding systems. Moreover, GPT has sparked interest in the research community and inspired further advancements in language modeling and generation. Overall, GPT represents a significant milestone in NLP, pushing the boundaries of what is achievable in language understanding and generation tasks and paving the way for more sophisticated and capable language models in the future.

Here's a list of tasks that GPT models, like GPT-3 and GPT-4, can perform across different domains:

1. Text Generation:
   - Creative writing (stories, poems, etc.)
   - Content creation (articles, blogs, etc.)
   - Dialogue generation
2. Text Completion:
   - Sentence completion
   - Paragraph completion
   - Text summarization
3. Translation:
   - Language translation (e.g., English to French, Spanish to English)
   - Text localization
4. Question Answering:
   - General knowledge questions
   - Fact-based queries
   - FAQs
5. Programming Assistance:
   - Code generation (e.g., Python, JavaScript)
   - Code debugging
   - Code comments/documentation
6. Data Analysis:
   - Data summarization

- Data visualization descriptions
- Basic statistical analysis explanations

7. Content Recommendations:
   - Product recommendations
   - Book/movie/music suggestions
   - Learning resources recommendations
8. Educational Assistance:
   - Homework help
   - Study guides
   - Tutoring (basic explanations and clarifications)
9. Conversation:
   - Chatbots
   - Customer support automation
   - Interactive storytelling
10. Simulation:
    - Scenario generation
    - Role-playing game narratives
    - Virtual world descriptions
11. Personal Productivity:
    - To-do list management
    - Reminder setting
    - Note-taking
12. Accessibility:
    - Text-to-speech conversion

- Speech-to-text conversion
- Simplifying complex text

13. Creative Projects:
    - Idea brainstorming
    - Concept generation
    - Plot development
14. Financial Analysis:
    - Basic financial report summaries
    - Investment suggestions (general advice)
15. Health and Wellness:
    - Symptom checker (general advice)
    - Basic nutrition and exercise tips

These are just some examples of the wide range of tasks that GPT models can handle. The versatility of GPT makes it a powerful tool across various industries and applications, pushing the boundaries of what's possible in natural language processing and AI-driven text generation.

OpenAI has released several versions of the GPT model over time, each with its own improvements and advancements. Here's an overview of the various versions of GPT and their key differences:

Table 14: GPT Evolution

Version	Release Year	Parameters	Notable Features
GPT	2018	110M	Base model
GPT-2	2019	1.5B	Multi-layer, no fine-tuning
GPT-2.5	2019	1.5B	Safety updates
GPT-3	2020	175B	Scaling up, fine-tuning
GPT-3.5	2020	175B	Enhanced safety and efficiency
GPT-4	2022	*have not been officially disclosed*	

In the realm of artificial intelligence and natural language processing, the GPT series by OpenAI has undeniably reshaped our understanding of what machines can achieve with language. From the groundbreaking release of GPT in 2018 to the advanced capabilities of GPT-3.5, these models have demonstrated remarkable progress in generating coherent and contextually relevant text. While GPT-4 and other models from various organizations continue to push the boundaries of AI capabilities, it's clear that we are witnessing an era of unprecedented innovation in language-based AI technologies. As we look ahead, the evolution of GPT and its successors promises to further transform industries, enrich user experiences, and challenge our perceptions of AI's potential in the years to come.

3.3.6 XLNet

XLNet (eXtreme Learning Machine Network) is a state-of-the-art language model developed by researchers at Google that builds upon the transformer architecture and introduces several innovative techniques to improve language representation learning. Unlike previous models that rely solely on autoregressive language modeling, XLNet incorporates the permutation language modeling objective, which allows it to capture bidirectional context information more effectively. This objective randomly masks tokens in the input sequence and predicts them based on both left and right context, enabling XLNet to learn from all possible permutations of the input sequence.

Let’s understand with the example,

Sentence: "The sun shines brightly in the sky."
Input sequence with masked tokens: "The [MASK] shines [MASK] in the [MASK]."

XLNet will predict the masked tokens by considering the context from both the left and right sides.

Possible predictions could be:

1. "The sun shines brightly in the sky."
2. "The sky shines brightly in the sun."
3. "The sun shines brightly in the clouds."

XLNet considers all possible permutations of the input sequence to capture bidirectional context effectively, enabling it to understand the relationships between words and generate accurate predictions.

By leveraging the permutation language modeling objective, XLNet is able to overcome limitations associated with traditional autoregressive language models, such as the exposure bias problem and the inability to capture bidirectional context. This approach enables XLNet to generate more accurate and contextually rich representations of language, leading to improvements in various NLP tasks. Moreover, XLNet achieves state-of-the-art performance on benchmark datasets across a wide range of tasks, including text classification, question answering, and language understanding.

XLNet has garnered attention in the research community and inspired advancements in language representation learning. It can capture bidirectional context information while retaining the benefits of autoregressive language modeling. This ability has led to major improvements in tasks related to understanding and generating language. XLNet has also shown resilience against changes in domains and attacks from adversaries, making it useful for practical applications.

Overall, XLNet marks a significant step forward in NLP. It expands the possibilities in language representation learning and sets the stage for more advanced and capable language models in the future.

------------------- *End of chapter 3* -------------------

4 Machine Learning Basics

In the area of NLP, Machine Learning (ML) serves as a cornerstone, enabling systems to automatically learn from data and make predictions or decisions without explicit programming. In this chapter, we go on a journey through the fundamental concepts of Machine Learning, exploring its relevance, methodologies, and applications in the context of NLP. From classification and regression to clustering and deep learning, Machine Learning offers a diverse array of techniques that empower NLP systems to extract insights, understand language patterns, and generate meaningful responses.

Machine Learning, at its core, involves algorithms that iteratively learn from data, identifying patterns and making predictions or decisions based on the learned patterns. In the context of NLP, Machine Learning algorithms can analyse large volumes of text data, learn the relationships between words and phrases, and generate models that can understand and produce human-like text. This chapter aims to unravel the underlying principles of Machine Learning and demonstrate how they can be applied to solve various language processing tasks.

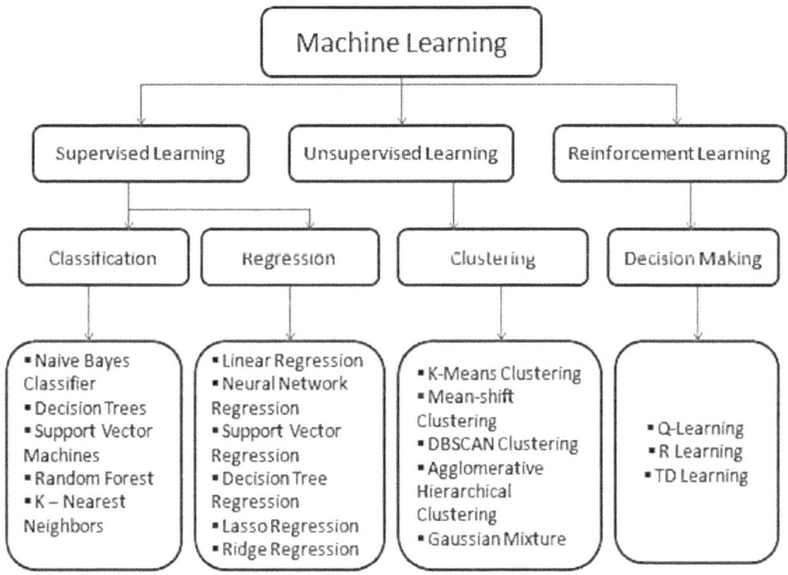

Figure 9: Machine Learning Algorithms Classification[6]

Throughout this chapter, we will delve into the essential concepts of Machine Learning, including supervised learning, unsupervised learning, and reinforcement learning. We will explore different algorithms used with NLP, such as Support Vector Machines (SVM), Naive Bayes (NB), Decision Trees (DT), Random Forest (RF) , K-Nearest Neighbour (KNN) and Neural Networks (NN), discussing their strengths, weaknesses, and practical applications. By gaining a solid understanding of Machine Learning basics,

[6] Image source : https://cdn-images-1.medium.com/max/800/1*rbaxTrB_CZCqbty_zv2bEg.png

readers will be equipped with the knowledge to harness the power of data-driven approaches in NLP and build intelligent language processing systems.

4.1 Types of ML Algorithms

Supervised learning, unsupervised learning, semi-supervised learning, and reinforcement learning are fundamental paradigms in machine learning, each offering unique approaches to learning from data and making predictions or decisions. In this section, we delve into these learning paradigms and their applications in NLP, exploring how they enable machines to understand and process human language effectively.

4.1.1 Supervised learning

Supervised learning involves training a model on labeled data, where each input is associated with a corresponding output or target label. The goal is to learn a mapping from input features to output labels, allowing the model to make predictions on unseen data. In NLP, supervised learning is widely used for tasks such as text classification, sentiment analysis, named entity recognition, and machine translation. By learning from labeled examples, supervised learning algorithms can capture the relationships between linguistic features and their corresponding labels, enabling accurate prediction on new text data.

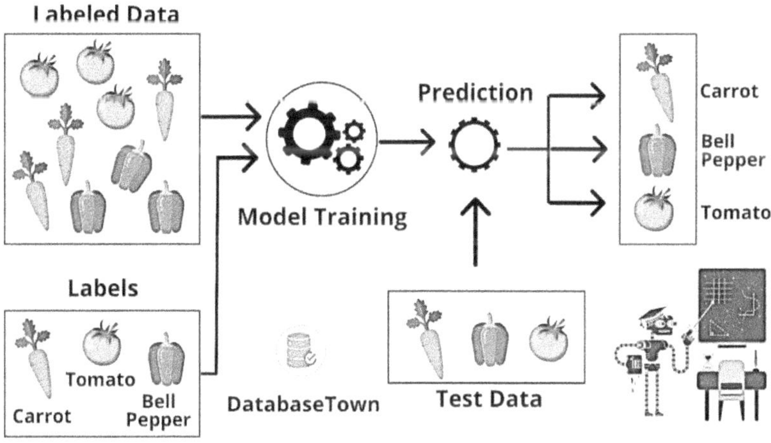

Figure 10: Supervised Machine Learning Model[7]

Example

<u>Sentiment Analysis</u>

Below is a simplified example illustrating the supervised learning process for text classification using a small dataset with five records.

[7] Image source : https://media.licdn.com/dms/image/D4D12AQGrJh_Y_FEcNg/article-inline_image-shrink_1500_2232/0/1694573153162?e=1718841600&v=beta&t=0jgsBBCiRB_EoMppzrTPOq4e2UXHvkCxSRHPmtq-l1c

The task is to classify customer reviews into two categories: "Positive" and "Negative".

Dataset

ID	Text	Label
1	This product is excellent!	Positive
2	I do not recommend this product.	Negative
3	The service was great, I will come back again.	Positive
4	Terrible experience with this company.	Negative
5	The quality of the product is poor.	Negative

Training and Testing

Training Data (4 records)

Text	Label
This product is excellent!	Positive
I do not recommend this product.	Negative
The service was great, I will come back again.	Positive
Terrible experience with this company.	Negative

Testing Data (1 record)

Text	Actual Label	Predicted Label
The quality of the product is poor.	Negative	?

Steps:

1. Data Preprocessing:
    a. Convert text to lowercase.

   b. Tokenize the text.
   c. Remove punctuation and stop words.
2. Feature Extraction:
   a. Convert text to numerical vectors using TF-IDF or word embeddings.
3. Model Training:
   a. Train a machine learning model (e.g., Logistic Regression, Naive Bayes) on the training data.
4. Prediction:
   a. Use the trained model to predict labels for the testing data.

Example Prediction:

After training the model, let's say it predicts the following label for the testing data:

Text	Actual Label	Predicted Label
The quality of the product is poor.	Negative	Negative

In this example, the model correctly predicts the label "Negative" for the test record "The quality of the product is poor.", indicating that it has learned the relationship between the text features and the corresponding labels from the training data.

Here it shows 100% accuracy of a ML model.

Let's understand what is the meaning of accuracy:

Table 15 : Accuracy of Various Models Based on Training and Testing Records

Model	Training Records	Testing Records	Correct Predictions	Accuracy
Model A	800	200	190	95%
Model B	1000	250	225	90%
Model C	1200	300	285	95%
Model D	1500	400	360	90%
Model E	900	100	85	85%

This table shows the number of training and testing dummy records for each model, along with the number of correct predictions on the testing set and the corresponding accuracy.

4.1.2 Unsupervised learning

Unsupervised learning, on the other hand, involves training a model on unlabeled data, where the goal is to discover hidden patterns or structures within the data. In NLP, unsupervised learning techniques such as clustering, topic modeling, and word embeddings are used to uncover semantic relationships between words, group similar documents together, and extract latent topics from text corpora. Unsupervised learning algorithms enable machines to automatically learn from raw text data without the need for annotated labels, making them valuable tools for exploring and analysing large-scale textual datasets.

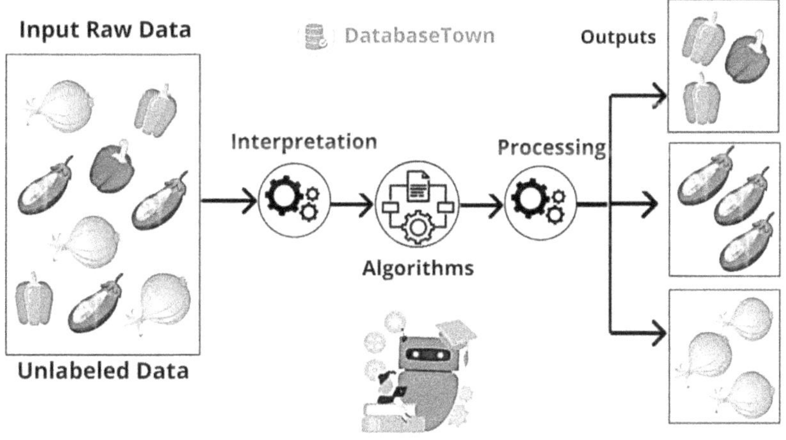

Figure 11: Unsupervised Machine Learning Model[8]

Example

Let's consider the task of topic modeling using unsupervised lcarning as an example in NLP.

Task: Topic Modeling
Objective: Discover hidden topics or themes within a collection of documents.

[8] Image Source : https://databasetown.com/wp-content/uploads/2023/05/Unsupervised-Learning.jpg

Suppose we have a collection of documents related to technology, sports, and health. We want to identify the main topics or themes present in these documents without any predefined labels.

Documents:

1. "The new smartphone features advanced AI capabilities and a stunning display."
2. "The football match was intense, with both teams giving their best performance."
3. "Regular exercise and a balanced diet are essential for maintaining good health."
4. "The latest software update enhances user experience with improved performance."
5. "Athletes follow strict training routines to achieve peak performance in competitions."

Unsupervised Learning Process for Topic Modeling

1. Data Preprocessing:
    a. Tokenization
    b. Removing stop words
    c. Stemming/Lemmatization
2. Feature Extraction:
    a. Convert the preprocessed text into numerical vectors using techniques like TF-IDF or word embeddings.

3. Topic Modeling:
    a. Apply unsupervised learning algorithms like Latent Dirichlet Allocation (LDA) or Non-Negative Matrix Factorization (NMF) to discover latent topics within the document collection.
4. Interpretation of Topics:
    a. Analyze the top words associated with each identified topic to interpret and label them based on the word distributions.

Example Output from Topic Modeling

Suppose after applying topic modeling, we obtain the following topics and their associated keywords:

- Topic 1: Technology
    - Keywords: smartphone, AI, display, software, update
- Topic 2: Sports
    - Keywords: football, match, athletes, training, competitions
- Topic 3: Health
    - Keywords: exercise, diet, health, balanced, maintaining

Interpretation

Based on the identified topics and keywords, we can infer that:

- Topic 1 mainly relates to Technology.
- Topic 2 focuses on Sports.
- Topic 3 is related to Health.

By applying unsupervised learning techniques like topic modeling, we can automatically discover and categorize the main themes or topics present in a collection of documents, making it easier to analyse and understand large textual datasets without manual labeling.

4.1.3 Semi-supervised learning

Semi-supervised learning lies between supervised and unsupervised learning, combining labeled and unlabeled data to improve model performance. In NLP, semi-supervised learning techniques leverage a small amount of labeled data along with a large pool of unlabeled data to train models that generalize well to unseen examples. Semi-supervised learning algorithms are particularly useful in scenarios where labeled data is scarce or expensive to acquire, allowing machines to leverage the abundance of unlabeled data available in many NLP applications.

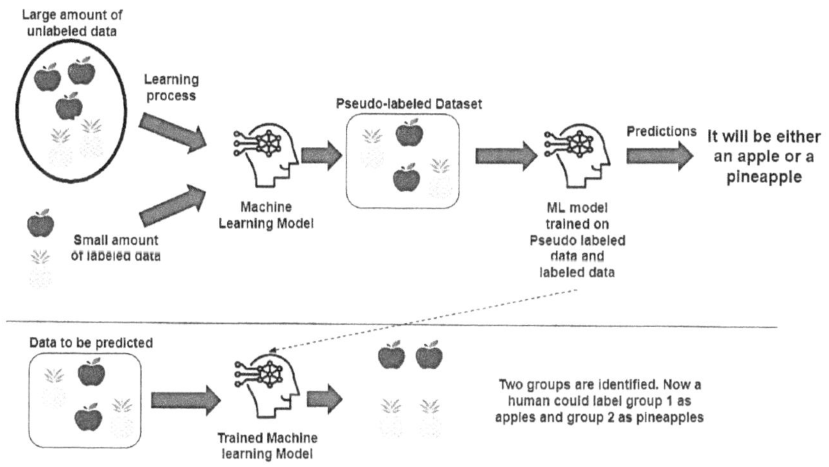

Figure 12: Semi-Supervised Machine Learning Model[9]

Example

Problem: Email Spam Classification

Data:

- Labeled Data (50 emails):
    - 25 emails labeled as "spam"
    - 25 emails labeled as "not spam"
- Unlabeled Data (950 emails)

Approach:

[9] Image Source - https://miro.medium.com/v2/resize:fit:1400/1*CzVENZj3bWrwhRBN4hQq7Q.png

- **Labeled Data:** Train a classifier using the 50 labeled emails. For instance, a supervised learning algorithm like Logistic Regression, Decision Trees, or Support Vector Machines can be used.
- **Pseudo-labeling:**
    - Use the trained classifier to predict labels for the 950 unlabeled emails.
    - Assign a label to each email based on the highest predicted probability. For instance, if an email has a 70% probability of being "spam", it's labeled as "spam".
- **Combine Labeled and Pseudo-labeled Data:**
    - Combine the 50 labeled emails with the 950 pseudo-labeled emails to form a larger dataset of 1000 emails.
- **Retrain the Classifier:**
    - Use this combined dataset to retrain the classifier.

Advantages

- Utilizes Unlabeled Data: The vast amount of unlabeled data helps improve the model's generalization and performance.
- Cost-effective: It reduces the need for extensive labeled data, which can be expensive and time-consuming to acquire.

Disadvantages

- Pseudo-labeling Errors: Incorrectly labeled data can negatively impact model performance.
- Dependency on Initial Model: The quality of the initial model can influence the performance of the semi-supervised learning process.

This example illustrates the basic idea behind semi-supervised learning. In practice, various techniques and algorithms can be employed to leverage both labeled and unlabeled data effectively.

4.1.4 Reinforcement learning

Reinforcement learning is a learning paradigm where an agent learns to interact with an environment by taking actions and receiving feedback in the form of rewards or penalties. In NLP, reinforcement learning is used for tasks such as dialogue systems, machine translation, and text generation, where the agent learns to generate human-like responses by maximizing a reward signal. Reinforcement learning algorithms enable machines to learn complex language tasks through trial and error, gradually improving performance through experience and feedback.

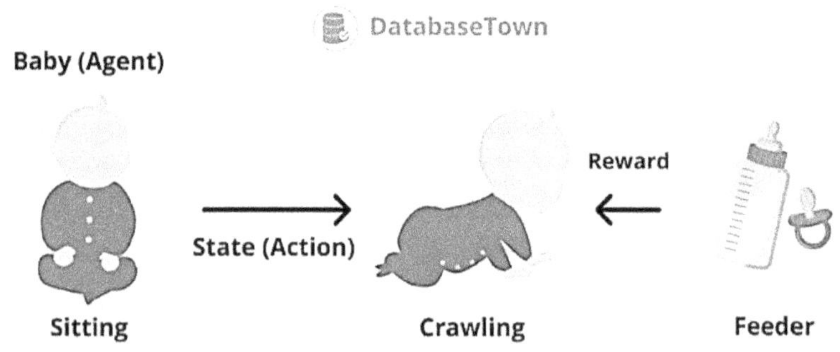

Figure 13: Reinforcement Learning Example[10]

Let's understand the image :

Scenario: Baby and Milk Bottle

Environment: The baby's surroundings, including the milk bottle.

Agent: The baby

Objective: The baby aims to reach the milk bottle and drink milk.

Reward System:

- +1 for successfully reaching and drinking from the milk bottle.
- -1 for any unsafe behaviour or failure to reach the milk bottle.
- +0 for idle actions or waiting without attempting to reach the milk bottle.

[10] Image Source : https://databasetown.com/wp-content/uploads/2023/05/Reinforcement-Learning-1024x726.jpg

Training Process

1. Initialization: The baby starts in a sitting position, noticing the milk bottle.
2. Interaction: The baby observes the milk bottle and decides to take action.
3. Action Selection: The baby attempts to crawl, reach, or grab the milk bottle.
4. Feedback: The baby receives a reward based on the outcome of the action.
5. Learning: The baby learns from the feedback to adjust future actions.

Example Interaction

1. Observation: The baby notices the milk bottle placed a short distance away.
2. Decision: The baby decides to try crawling towards the milk bottle.
3. Action: The baby starts crawling towards the milk bottle.
4. Outcome:
    a. If the baby successfully reaches and drinks from the milk bottle: Reward: +1
    b. If the baby stops or changes direction without reaching the milk bottle: Reward: -1

c. If the baby waits without attempting to move: Reward: +0

Training Outcome

Through repeated attempts and feedback, the baby learns to coordinate its movements better, improve crawling skills, and successfully reach the milk bottle to drink milk. Over time, the baby becomes more efficient in reaching the desired object, demonstrating learning and adaptation through trial and error, which is a fundamental concept of reinforcement learning.

This scenario illustrates how basic reinforcement learning principles can be applied to understand and analyze the learning process in young infants as they explore and interact with their environment to achieve specific goals.

- In the Subway Surfers game, the player character, such as Jake or Tricky, navigates through a dynamic subway environment filled with tracks, obstacles, coins, and power-ups.
- The player's objective is to run as far as possible, collecting coins, avoiding obstacles, and utilizing power-ups to achieve a high score.
- The game employs a reward system to provide feedback on the player's actions: collecting coins yields a reward of +1 , hitting

obstacles results in a penalty of -1 , and successfully using power-ups grants a reward of +5.

- During gameplay, the player continuously observes the game environment, makes decisions to control movements (e.g., jump, slide, move left/right), and receives rewards or penalties based on the outcomes of these actions.
- Over time, through trial and error, the player learns to anticipate obstacles, strategically use power-ups, and optimize gameplay strategies to progress further and achieve higher scores.
- This learning process exemplifies the principles of reinforcement learning, where continuous feedback drives adaptation and improvement in gameplay performance.

Example

- Imagine a sentiment analysis model tasked with categorizing user-generated text into positive, negative, or neutral sentiments.
- Initialized with basic language understanding capabilities, the model interacts with a dataset comprising user reviews or social media comments.
- Upon receiving an input text, the model predicts the sentiment label and receives feedback based on the accuracy of its prediction.
- For correct classifications,
    - the model earns a reward of +1, while

  - misclassifications incur a penalty of -1
  - Ambiguous cases, such as texts with neutral sentiments or those difficult to classify, result in a neutral reward of +0
- Over time, through continuous interactions and feedback-driven learning, the sentiment analysis model refines its language understanding capabilities, enabling it to discern sentiment nuances more accurately and provide precise sentiment classifications.

This iterative learning process exemplifies the power of reinforcement learning in training NLP models to effectively analyze and interpret human-generated text, facilitating applications in social media monitoring, customer feedback analysis, and opinion mining.

In summary, supervised learning, unsupervised learning, semi-supervised learning, and reinforcement learning are essential paradigms in machine learning, each offering unique approaches to learning from data and solving language-related tasks in NLP. By understanding the principles and applications of these learning paradigms, researchers and practitioners can leverage their strengths to build intelligent language processing systems that can understand, interpret, and generate human-like text with remarkable accuracy and fluency.

4.2 Machine Learning Classifiers

This chapter serves as a comprehensive guide to understanding machine learning classifiers and their applications in NLP. This chapter is designed to provide readers with a solid foundation in the principles, methodologies, and implementations of binary and multiclass classifiers, enabling them to effectively utilize these techniques in various language processing tasks.

The chapter begins with an overview of binary classifiers, which are algorithms that classify input instances into one of two classes or categories. Examples of binary classification tasks in NLP include sentiment analysis (positive or negative sentiment), spam detection (spam or non-spam), and language identification (English or non-English). Readers will learn about popular binary classifiers such as Logistic Regression, Support Vector Machines , Naive Bayes, Decision Trees, and Random Forests, along with their strengths, weaknesses, and practical applications in NLP.

Following the discussion on binary classifiers, the chapter progresses to multiclass classifiers, which extend the concept of binary classification to scenarios where input instances can belong to more than two classes or categories. Multiclass classification tasks in NLP include document classification (assigning documents to multiple topics or categories), part-of-speech tagging (assigning each word in a sentence to its grammatical category), and named entity recognition (identifying and classifying entities such as persons, organizations, and locations). Readers will explore various multiclass classifiers, including Multinomial Naive Bayes, Support Vector Machines, Decision Trees, and Neural Networks, and gain insights into their applications and performance considerations in NLP.

In this chapter, we briefly touch upon the basics of machine learning, a vast and intricate field that forms the backbone of many artificial intelligence applications, including natural language processing. While machine learning encompasses a wide range of algorithms and methodologies, our focus here is to provide readers with a foundational understanding to appreciate its relevance in the context of NLP.

However, it's important to note that this overview is intended to offer a glimpse into the world of machine learning rather than an exhaustive exploration. Due to the depth and complexity of the subject, a comprehensive discussion would extend beyond the scope of this book. For those interested in delving deeper into machine learning, there are numerous specialized resources and textbooks available that offer detailed insights and practical applications.

4.2.1 Logistic Regression

Logistic Regression is a widely used binary classification algorithm in NLP that models the probability of a binary outcome based on one or more predictor variables. Despite its name, logistic regression is a classification algorithm rather than a regression algorithm. In NLP,

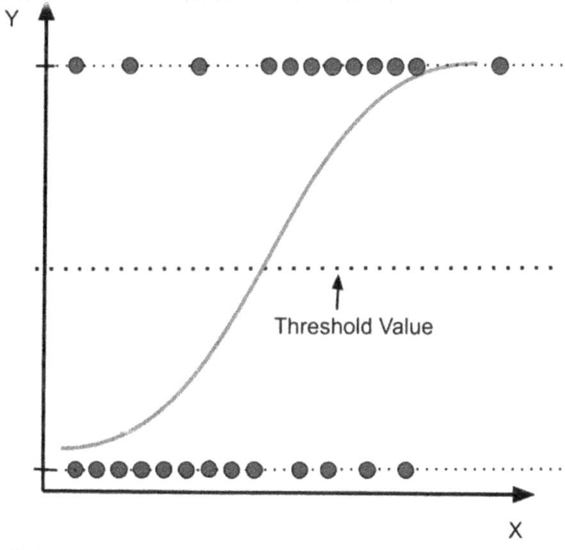

Figure 14: Logistic Regression[11]

[11] Image Source : https://miro.medium.com/v2/resize:fit:1400/1*KZQYpR-aWsSF2Zl7JFRI5A.png

logistic regression is commonly used for tasks such as sentiment analysis, spam detection, and text categorization. The algorithm learns a linear decision boundary between the classes by optimizing a logistic loss function, which measures the discrepancy between predicted probabilities and actual class labels.

Mathematical Foundation

The logistic regression model uses the logistic function (also known as the sigmoid function) to map any input into a value between 0 and 1. The sigmoid function is defined as:

$$\sigma(z) = \frac{1}{1+e^{-z}}$$

Where 'z' is the linear combination of the input features and their corresponding weights:

$$z = w_0 + w_1x_1 + w_2x_2 + \ldots + w_nx_n$$

Here, $w0, w_1, w_2, \ldots, w_n$ are the model parameters (weights), and $x_1, x_2, \ldots, x_n$ are the input features.

Prediction

The output of the logistic function represents the probability that the given input belongs to the positive class (class 1). For binary classification:

$$P(Y = 1|X) = \sigma(z)$$
$$P(Y = 0|X) = 1 - \sigma(z)$$

Training

The goal during training is to find the optimal values for the weights $w_0, w_1, \ldots, w_n$ that minimize the difference between the predicted probabilities and the actual labels in the training data.

This is typically done using an optimization algorithm like *gradient descent*, where the objective is to minimize the logistic loss (or cross-entropy loss) function:

$$J(w) = -\frac{1}{N} \sum_{i=1}^{N} [y_i \log(\hat{y}_i) + (1 - y_i) \log(1 - \hat{y}_i)]$$

Here, N is the number of training samples, y_i is the actual label (0 or 1) for the ith sample, and $y\hat{}i$ is the predicted probability for the ith sample.

Logistic regression is favoured for its simplicity, interpretability, and efficiency, making it a popular choice for binary classification tasks, especially when the number of features is large or when interpretability is essential.

4.2.2 Support Vector Machine

Support Vector Machine (SVM) is a powerful binary classification algorithm that aims to find the optimal hyperplane that separates instances of different classes with the maximum margin. In NLP, SVMs are commonly used for text classification tasks, such as sentiment analysis, document categorization, and spam detection. SVMs work by mapping input instances into a high-dimensional feature space and finding the hyperplane that best separates the classes.

The algorithm aims to maximize the margin between the classes while minimizing classification errors. SVMs are known for their ability to handle high-dimensional data, handle non-linear decision boundaries through kernel tricks, and achieve robust performance in various NLP tasks. However, SVMs can be sensitive to the choice of kernel function and require careful parameter tuning to achieve optimal performance.

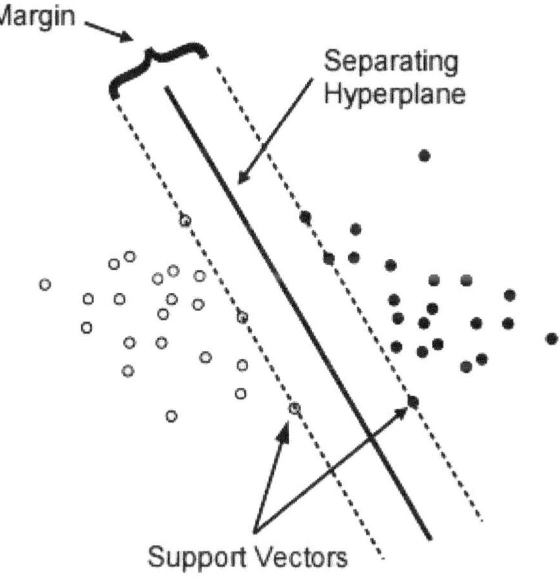

Figure 15: Support Vector Machine[12]

The primary goal of an SVM is to find the hyperplane that best separates the data into different classes.

Here's a step-by-step breakdown of how SVMs work for classification:

[12] Image Source : https://media.licdn.com/dms/image/D4D12AQG-yCCKvlI2zw/article-cover_image-shrink_600_2000/0/1654882185622?e=2147483647&v=beta&t=c0azA2BUiSGxwejZk7kF2N0Lp-7lPtjusu2VmN2VDn0

1. Data Preparation: Start with a dataset where each data point belongs to one of two classes. Each data point is represented by a feature vector.

2. Feature Space: SVM maps the input data into a high-dimensional feature space. In this space, data points are represented as points and the goal is to find a hyperplane that separates these points into classes as distinctly as possible.

3. Finding the Hyperplane: The hyperplane in SVM is the decision boundary that best separates the classes. The "best" hyperplane is the one that maximizes the margin between the closest data points (support vectors) from each class.

4. Support Vectors: Support vectors are the data points that lie closest to the hyperplane. These points are crucial as they define the decision boundary and the margin.

5. Kernel Trick: In cases where the data is not linearly separable, SVM uses a kernel trick to map the data into a higher-dimensional space where it becomes linearly separable. Common kernel functions include linear, polynomial, radial basis function (RBF), and sigmoid.

6. Optimization: The optimization problem in SVM involves finding the parameters of the hyperplane (weights and bias)

that minimize the classification error and maximize the margin. This is typically solved using optimization techniques like *Quadratic* Programming.

7. Classification: Once the hyperplane is determined, you can classify new data points by simply determining on which side of the hyperplane they fall.

Mathematical Foundation

Given a training dataset $\{(x1,y1),(x2,y2),...,(xn,yn)\}$, where xi is the feature vector and yi is the class label ($yi \in \{-1,1\}$), the goal of SVM is to find the optimal hyperplane that separates the data into two classes while maximizing the margin.

The hyperplane is represented by the equation:

$$w \cdot x + b = 0$$

Where:

- w is the weight vector perpendicular to the hyperplane.
- b is the bias term.
- x is the feature vector.

The distance between the hyperplane and the closest data point from either class is known as the margin. The goal is to maximize this margin.

The optimization problem for SVM can be formulated as:

$$\text{Minimize } \frac{1}{2}||w||^2$$

Subject to the constraints:

$$y_i(w \cdot x_i + b) \geq 1 \text{ for all } i = 1, 2, ..., n$$

Here:

$||w||$ represents the Euclidean norm of the weight vector w.

- The term $yi(w{\cdot}xi{+}b)$ ensures that each data point is correctly classified by the hyperplane.
- The constraint $yi(w{\cdot}xi{+}b){\geq}1$ ensures that the data points lie outside the margin.

To handle cases where the data is not linearly separable, SVM introduces the concept of slack variables ξi. The optimization problem becomes:

$$\text{Minimize } \frac{1}{2}||w||^2 + C\sum_{i=1}^{n} \xi_i$$

Subject to:

$$y_i(w \cdot x_i + b) \geq 1 - \xi_i \text{ and } \xi_i \geq 0 \text{ for all } i = 1, 2, ..., n$$

Where:

- C is a regularization parameter that controls the trade-off between maximizing the margin and minimizing classification error. A larger C value means a smaller margin but potentially better classification accuracy.

This formulation allows for some misclassification (controlled by ξi – slack variable) to achieve a better overall margin.

The symbol ξ (xi) is pronounced as "ksi" or "zai." It is a letter in the Greek alphabet. The pronunciation can vary slightly depending on the context and regional accents, but "ksi" (rhyming with "sky") is a common pronunciation in mathematical and scientific contexts.

Once the optimization problem is solved, the weight vector w and bias term b are used to classify new data points using the decision function:

$$f(x) = \text{sign}(w \cdot x + b)$$

Where:

sign is the sign function that returns +1 or −1 based on the value of $w \cdot x + b$.

This is a simplified explanation of the mathematical formulation of SVM for linear classification. SVMs can also be extended to handle non-linear classification using kernel functions, but that involves a more complex optimization problem.

4.2.3 Naive Bayes

Naive Bayes is a probabilistic binary classification algorithm based on Bayes' theorem, which calculates the probability of a class given the observed features. Despite its simplicity and "naive" assumption of feature independence, Naive Bayes classifiers perform surprisingly well in many NLP tasks, including sentiment analysis, spam filtering, and text classification. In NLP, Naive Bayes models are often used for their efficiency, scalability, and ease of implementation. The algorithm computes the conditional probability of each class given the input features and selects the class with the highest probability as the predicted class. Naive Bayes classifiers are particularly suitable for text classification tasks with a large number of features, such as bag-of-words representations, where feature independence assumption holds reasonably well.

Example

Suppose we have a dataset with two features, Weather and Temperature, and we want to predict whether people will play tennis.

Dataset

Weather	Temperature	Play Tennis
Sunny	Hot	No
Overcast	Mild	Yes
Rainy	Cool	Yes
Sunny	Mild	Yes
Rainy	Hot	No

Let's calculate the probabilities to predict whether people will play tennis given that the Weather is Sunny and the Temperature is Mild.

Calculate Prior Probabilities

P(Play Tennis=Yes) and *P*(Play Tennis=No)

$$P(\text{Play Tennis} = \text{Yes}) = \frac{3}{5}$$
$$P(\text{Play Tennis} = \text{No}) = \frac{2}{5}$$

Calculate Likelihood Probabilities for each feature

$$P(\text{Weather} = \text{Sunny}|\text{Play Tennis} = \text{Yes})$$
$$P(\text{Temperature} = \text{Mild}|\text{Play Tennis} = \text{Yes})$$

$$P(\text{Weather} = \text{Sunny}|\text{Play Tennis} = \text{Yes}) = \frac{2}{3}$$
$$P(\text{Temperature} = \text{Mild}|\text{Play Tennis} = \text{Yes}) = \frac{2}{3}$$

Calculate Posterior Probabilities

$$P(\text{Play Tennis} = \text{Yes}|\text{Weather} = \text{Sunny}, \text{Temperature} = \text{Mild})$$

Using the Naive Bayes formula

$$P(Y|X) = \frac{P(X|Y) \times P(Y)}{P(X)}$$

$$P(\text{Play Tennis} = \text{Yes}|\text{Weather} = \text{Sunny}, \text{Temperature} = \text{Mild})$$
$$= \frac{P(\text{Weather=Sunny}|\text{Play Tennis=Yes}) \times P(\text{Temperature=Mild Play Tennis=Yes}) \times P(\text{Play Tennis=Yes})}{P(\text{Weather=Sunny}) \times P(\text{Temperature=Mild})}$$

$$= \frac{\frac{2}{3} \times \frac{2}{3} \times \frac{3}{5}}{\frac{3}{5} \times \frac{3}{5}}$$

$$= \frac{100}{135}$$

$$\approx 0.7407$$

So, the probability of playing tennis given that the Weather is Sunny and the Temperature is Mild is approximately 0.7407.

However, Naive Bayes classifiers may suffer from the issue of zero probabilities for unseen features and may not capture complex relationships between features. Nonetheless, they remain a popular choice for binary classification tasks in NLP due to their simplicity and effectiveness.

4.2.4 Decision Tree

Decision Trees are versatile binary classification algorithms that recursively partition the feature space into regions based on simple decision rules inferred from the training data. In NLP, decision trees are commonly used for tasks such as text classification, sentiment analysis, and named entity recognition. Decision Trees aim to maximize information gain or minimize impurity at each split, leading to a tree structure where each internal node represents a decision based on a feature, and each leaf node represents a class label. Decision Trees are known for their interpretability, ease of visualization, and ability to handle both numerical and categorical features. However, Decision Trees can suffer from overfitting, especially when the tree depth is too large or when the training data is noisy. Ensemble methods like Random Forests are often used to mitigate overfitting and improve classification performance.

Overfitting

Overfitting occurs when a machine learning model learns the training data too well, capturing noise or random fluctuations in the data as if they were meaningful patterns. This results in a model that performs very well on the training data but fails to generalize to new, unseen data. Essentially, the model has memorized the training data rather than learning the underlying patterns that would enable it to make accurate predictions on new data. Overfitting is a common problem in machine learning, particularly when the model is too complex relative to the amount of training data available. It can be addressed through techniques such as cross-validation, regularization, and using simpler models.

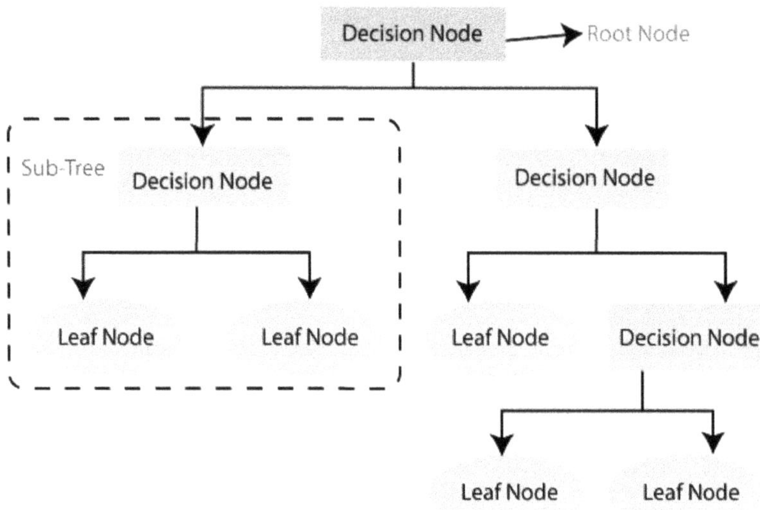

Figure 16: Decision Tree[13]

Mathematical Formula

1. Splitting Criteria

At each node of the Decision Tree, the algorithm selects the best feature and the best split point for that feature to partition the data into two or more subsets. The goal is to minimize impurity (indicates the uncertainty in predicting the class or target value of a randomly chosen data point within that set) within each subset. Impurity is typically measured using metrics like *Gini impurity* or *entropy*.

[13] Image Source : https://static.javatpoint.com/tutorial/machine-learning/images/decision-tree-classification-algorithm.png

For classification problems, the splitting criteria often involve measures of impurity reduction such as:

- **Gini impurity (for classification):** It measures the probability of misclassifying a randomly chosen element if it were randomly labeled according to the distribution of labels in the subset.

$$Gini(X_m) = 1 - \sum_{k=1}^{K} p_{mk}^2$$

Where:

  - X_m is the subset of data at node m.
  - K is the number of classes.
  - p_{mk} is the proportion of data points in class k in subset X_m.

- **Entropy (for classification)**: It measures the average amount of information needed to classify a data point drawn from the distribution induced by the subset.

$$Entropy(X_m) = -\sum_{k=1}^{K} p_{mk} \log_2(p_{mk})$$

Where the terms are the same as in the Gini impurity formula.

- **Variance (for regression):** It measures the variability of the target variable within each subset.

2. Stopping Criteria

The decision tree-building process stops when one of the stopping criteria is met. This could be when all instances at a node belong to the same class, when the tree reaches a maximum depth, or when the number of instances at a node falls below a threshold.

Example

Let's say we have a dataset of customers and we want to build a Decision Tree to predict whether they will buy a product based on their age and income. Here's a simplified version of our dataset:

Age (years)	Income (k Rs)	Buy Product
30	50	Yes
40	40	No
25	70	Yes
35	55	Yes
50	45	No
45	60	Yes

1. Root Node
    a. The root node represents the entire dataset.
2. Select Splitting Feature and Criterion

   a. We need to choose the feature and criterion that best splits the dataset.
   b. Let's start with the feature "Age" and criterion Gini impurity.
3. Splitting the Root Node
   a. We'll split the dataset based on the age:
      i. If age < 40: Left branch
      ii. If age >= 40: Right branch
4. Left Branch (age < 40)
   a. Subset:

Age (years)	Income (k Rs)	Buy Product
30	50	Yes
25	70	Yes

   b. All instances in this subset have the same label ("Yes"), so this branch becomes a leaf node with the label "Yes".

5. Right Branch (age >= 40)
   a. Subset:

Age (years)	Income (k Rs)	Buy Product
40	40	No
35	55	Yes

50	45	No
45	60	Yes

b. We continue splitting this subset.

c. Let's choose the feature "Income" and criterion Gini impurity.

6. Splitting the Right Branch:

   a. If income < 50k: Left branch

   b. If income >= 50k: Right branch

7. Left Branch (income < 50k):

   a. Subset

Age (years)	Income (k Rs)	Buy Product
40	40	No
50	45	No

   b. All instances in this subset have the same label ("No"), so this branch becomes a leaf node with the label "No".

8. Right Branch (income >= 50k)

a. Subset

Age (years)	Income (k Rs)	Buy Product
35	55	Yes
45	60	Yes

b. All instances in this subset have the same label ("Yes"), so this branch becomes a leaf node with the label "Yes".

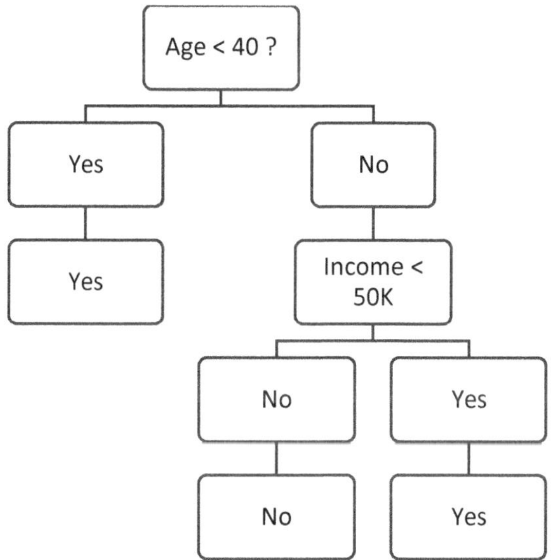

This is a simple Decision Tree that can be used to predict whether a customer will buy a product based on their age and income.

Overall, Decision Trees serve as a fundamental building block in the field of machine learning, providing a foundation for more advanced algorithms and techniques. Their intuitive nature and effectiveness make them a valuable tool for both beginners and experienced practitioners in the field of data science and predictive modeling.

4.2.5 Random Forest

Random Forest is an ensemble learning method that combines multiple Decision Trees to improve classification accuracy (a metric used to evaluate the performance of a machine learning model for classification tasks. It measures the proportion of correctly classified instances out of the total instances in the dataset) and robustness. In NLP, Random Forests are widely used for text classification, sentiment analysis, and spam detection. Random Forests work by training a collection of decision trees on bootstrap samples of the training data and aggregating their predictions through majority voting or averaging. This ensemble approach helps reduce overfitting and variance while capturing the complex relationships between features and classes. Random Forests are known for their robustness to noise and outliers (An outlier is a data point that is significantly different from the rest of the data. It stands out because it is much higher or lower than most of the other values), scalability to large datasets, and resistance to overfitting. They are often favored for binary classification tasks in NLP, especially when interpretability and performance are both important considerations.

Accuracy of Prediction Model

Mathematically, classification accuracy can be defined as:

*Accuracy = (Number of correctly classified instances / Total number of instances) * 100%*

For example, if a model correctly predicts 90 out of 100 instances in a dataset, the classification accuracy would be 90%.

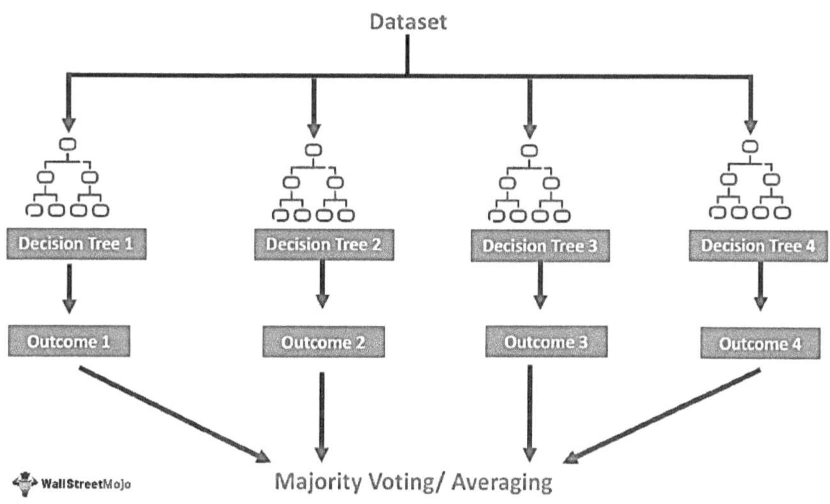

Figure 17: Random Forest[14]

The basic idea behind Random Forest is to build multiple decision trees during training and combine their predictions to obtain a more

[14] Image Source : https://www.wallstreetmojo.com/wp-content/uploads/2023/11/Random-Forest.png

accurate and stable prediction. Here's a simplified explanation of how Random Forest works along with an example:

1. **Decision Trees:** The Random Forest algorithm consists of multiple decision trees. Each decision tree is constructed based on a random subset of the training data and a random subset of features.

2. **Bootstrapping:** For each decision tree, a random subset of the training data is sampled with replacement. This process is called bootstrapping. Bootstrapping involves randomly selecting data points from the original dataset to create multiple subsets of data, each of which is used to train a decision tree.

3. **Random Feature Selection:** At each node of the decision tree, only a random subset of features is considered for splitting. This helps in reducing correlation between trees and making the ensemble more diverse.

4. **Voting or Averaging:** Once all the decision trees are built, predictions are made by each tree individually. For classification tasks, each tree "votes" for a class, and the class with the most votes becomes the final prediction. For regression tasks, the predictions of all trees are averaged to obtain the final prediction.

Example

Scenario : Predicting whether a customer will purchase a product based on demographic and behavioural features.

Here are the features:

- Age: Age of the customer.
- Income: Income level of the customer.
- Number of Purchases: Total number of purchases made by the customer.
- Website Visits: Number of visits to the company's website in the past month.

And the target variable is:

- Purchase: Whether the customer made a purchase (0 = No, 1 = Yes).

Now, let's see how Random Forest might work for this scenario:

1. **Bootstrapping:** Randomly select a subset of the training data (with replacement). Let's say we randomly select 70% of the customer data to train each decision tree.

2. **Random Feature Selection:** At each node of each decision tree, only a random subset of features is considered for splitting. For example, at the root node of the first tree, we

might consider features like Age, Income, and Website Visits for splitting.

3. **Build Decision Trees:** Construct multiple decision trees using the selected subsets of data and features. Each tree is trained independently of the others.

4. **Voting:** When making predictions for a new customer:

    a. Pass the customer through each decision tree to obtain individual predictions.

    b. For classification tasks:

        i. Count the votes for each class (Purchase or No Purchase). For instance,

            - if out of 10 trees,
            - 7 trees predict 'Purchase' and
            - 3 trees predict 'No Purchase',
            - the final prediction would be 'Purchase'.

    c. For regression tasks:

        i. Average the predictions from all decision trees to obtain the final prediction.

5. **Prediction:** Based on the voting or averaging, the final prediction for whether a customer will purchase a product is made.

By combining the strengths of multiple decision trees through ensemble learning, Random Forest can provide robust predictions, handle high-dimensional data, and effectively deal with noise and outliers. Its ability to mitigate overfitting, handle missing values, and capture complex relationships in the data makes it a popular choice for a wide range of real-world applications.

> Outliers are data points that significantly differ from other observations in a dataset. These observations are usually unusual, rare, or distinct from the majority of the data points. Outliers can arise due to various reasons, such as measurement errors, data corruption, or genuine but rare events in the phenomenon being observed.

In conclusion, Random Forest is a powerful and versatile machine learning algorithm that excels in both classification and regression tasks. Whether you're predicting customer behaviour, analysing financial data, or classifying medical images, Random Forest is a reliable and efficient tool in the machine learning toolkit.

4.2.6 K-Nearest Neighbours

K-Nearest Neighbours (KNN) is a non-parametric binary classification algorithm that classifies an input instance based on the majority class of its nearest neighbours in the feature space. In NLP, KNN is commonly used for tasks such as document classification, text categorization, and sentiment analysis. KNN works by calculating the distances between the input instance and all training instances in the feature space and selecting the *k* nearest neighbours based on a distance metric such as *Euclidean distance* or *cosine similarity*. The predicted class label is then determined by the majority class among the *k* nearest neighbours. KNN is known for its simplicity, flexibility, and ability to handle non-linear decision boundaries. However, KNN can be computationally expensive, especially with large datasets, and may suffer from the curse of dimensionality when the number of features is high.

Euclidean Distance

Euclidean distance is the "ordinary" straight-line distance between two points in Euclidean space. It's the distance between two points in a multidimensional space, calculated as the square root of the sum of the squares of the differences between corresponding coordinates.

In a 2-dimensional space with points (x_1,y_1) and (x_2,y_2), the Euclidean distance is calculated as:

Square root of $((x_2-x_1)^2 + (y_2-y_1)^2$

Manhattan Distance

Manhattan distance, also known as taxicab or city block distance, measures the distance between two points in a grid-based system. It's the sum of the absolute differences of their coordinates.

In a 2-dimensional space with points (x_1,y_1) and (x_2,y_2), the Manhattan distance is calculated as:

$| x_2-x_1 | + | y_2-y_1 |$

Example

Suppose we have a dataset of fruits with two features: weight (in grams) and colour (encoded as a numerical value, for example, 0 for red, 1 for yellow, and 2 for green). Each fruit in the dataset is labelled as either an apple or a banana.

Here is a small portion of the dataset:

Weight (grams)	Colour	Label
120	0	Apple
150	1	Apple
200	2	Banana
100	0	Apple
180	1	Banana

Now, suppose we want to classify a new fruit with a weight of 160 grams and colour yellow (colour code 1).

We'll use the k-NN algorithm to classify this new fruit:

1. **Calculate Distance:** Compute the distance between the new fruit and each fruit in the dataset. We can use the Euclidean distance formula:

$$\text{distance} = \sqrt{(x_2 - x_1)^2 + (y_2 - y_1)^2}$$

Where,

$x1,y1$ are the features of the new fruit (weight and colour) and $x2,y2$ are the features of each fruit in the dataset.

2. **Find Nearest Neighbours:** Select the *k* fruits in the dataset that are closest to the new fruit based on the calculated distances.

3. **Majority Vote:** Determine the majority class among the selected nearest neighbours. In this case, if most of the nearest neighbours are apples, we classify the new fruit as an apple; otherwise, we classify it as a banana.

For example, if we choose *k*=3 (a commonly used value):

- The three nearest neighbours to the new fruit (weight: 160 grams, colour: yellow) might be:
  - Fruit 1: Weight = 150 grams, Colour = 1 (Apple)
  - Fruit 2: Weight = 180 grams, Colour = 1 (Banana)
  - Fruit 3: Weight = 120 grams, Colour = 0 (Apple)

- Since two out of three nearest neighbours are apples, we classify the new fruit as an apple.

This is a basic example of how k-nearest neighbours can be applied for classification.

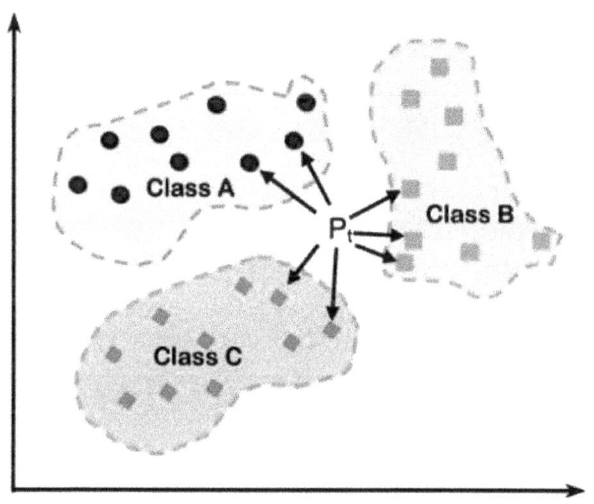

Figure 18: K- Nearest Neighbour[15]

Given a training dataset with labelled data points, the k-NN algorithm works as follows:

1. **Training Phase:** During the training phase, the algorithm simply stores all the training data.

[15] Image Source : https://miro.medium.com/v2/resize:fit:505/0*2_qzcm2gSe9l67al.png

2. **Prediction Phase:**

   a. For each new data point (the one we want to classify or regress), calculate its distance to all other data points in the training set. The distance metric commonly used is *Euclidean distance*, but other metrics like *Manhattan distance* or *Minkowski distance* can also be used.

   b. Identify the k-nearest data points (neighbours) to the new data point based on the calculated distances.

   c. For classification: Assign the class label that is most common among the k-nearest neighbours to the new data point.

   d. For regression: Take the average (or weighted average) of the target values of the k-nearest neighbours.

Mathematically, the algorithm can be summarized as follows:

1. For classification:

   a. Let D be the set of training data points.
   b. Given a new data point x, calculate the distance between x and each point in D.

   c. Select the k nearest neighbours of x from D.
   d. Assign the class label to x based on the majority class among the k nearest neighbours.
2. For regression:
   a. Let D be the set of training data points.
   b. Given a new data point x, calculate the distance between x and each point in D.
   c. Select the k nearest neighbours of x from D.
   d. Assign the target value to x as the average (or weighted average) of the target values of the k nearest neighbours.

The choice of k is crucial in the performance of the algorithm. A small k value can lead to overfitting, while a large k value can lead to underfitting. Typically, the optimal k value is determined through techniques such as cross-validation.

Cross-validation

Cross-validation is a technique used in machine learning and statistical modelling to assess how well a model will generalize to an independent dataset. It's primarily employed to evaluate the performance of a predictive model by partitioning the dataset into subsets, training the model on some of these subsets, and then evaluating it on the remaining data.

The basic idea behind cross-validation is to simulate the process of training and testing a model on multiple subsets of the data to obtain a more robust estimate of its performance. This helps to reduce the risk of overfitting, where the model learns to memorize the training data rather than capture underlying patterns that generalize well to unseen data.

Common cross-validation techniques include:

k-Fold Cross-Validation: The dataset is divided into k folds, and the model is trained and evaluated k times. Each time, a different fold is used as the validation set, and the rest are used for training.

Leave-One-Out Cross-Validation (LOOCV): Each data point is used as the validation set once, with k iterations where k is the number of data points. This is computationally expensive but provides a very accurate estimate of model performance.

Stratified Cross-Validation: Ensures that each fold maintains the same class distribution as the original dataset, which is particularly useful for imbalanced datasets.

It's important to note that the performance of k-NN heavily depends on the choice of the hyperparameter k and the distance metric used. Selecting the appropriate k value and distance metric through techniques like cross-validation is crucial to prevent overfitting or underfitting.

Moreover, while k-NN can work well with small to medium-sized datasets, its computational complexity grows linearly with the size of the training data, making it less efficient for large datasets.

In summary, KNN remains a valuable tool in the machine learning toolkit, particularly suitable for situations where interpretability and simplicity are prioritized, and the dataset size is manageable.

4.2.7 Other Binary Classifiers

Other binary classifiers commonly used in NLP include Linear Discriminant Analysis (LDA), Quadratic Discriminant Analysis (QDA), Gradient Boosting Machines (GBM), and Neural Networks. LDA and QDA are parametric classifiers that model the class-conditional probability distributions of the features, while GBM and Neural Networks are powerful ensemble and deep learning methods that can capture complex patterns in textual data. Each classifier has its strengths and weaknesses, and the choice of classifier depends on factors such as the nature of the data, the complexity of the problem, and the computational resources available.

4.2.8 Multi-Class Classifiers

Multiclass classifiers are machine learning algorithms designed to classify instances into one of multiple classes or categories. Unlike binary classifiers, which only distinguish between two classes, multiclass classifiers can handle scenarios where instances belong to more than two classes. In NLP, multiclass classifiers play a crucial role in tasks such as document classification, part-of-speech tagging, named entity recognition, and machine translation, where the number of possible classes exceeds two.

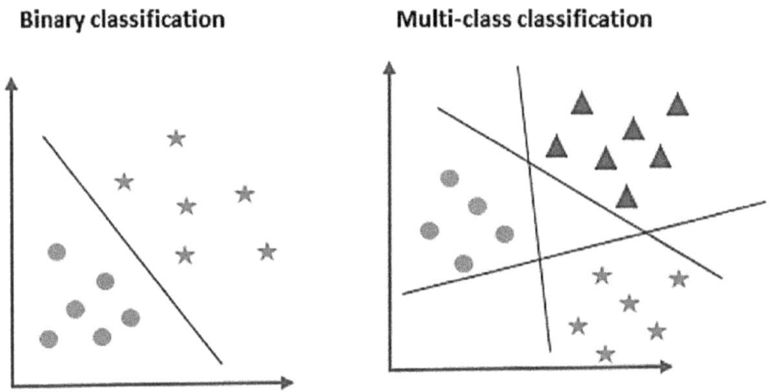

Figure 19: Binary Classification vs. Multiclass Classification[16]

One of the most common approaches to multiclass classification is the one-vs-all (OvA) strategy, also known as one-vs-rest. In this approach, a separate binary classifier is trained for each class, with the objective of distinguishing that class from all other classes. During prediction, the class with the highest confidence score from the individual binary classifiers is selected as the final predicted class. The OvA strategy is simple to implement and works well with most binary classifiers, making it a popular choice for multiclass classification tasks in NLP.

[16] Image Source : https://miro.medium.com/v2/resize:fit:725/1*nB6MM2qFvnsCDhSuhNPcLA.png

A **confidence score**, in the context of machine learning and classification tasks, represents the level of certainty or probability that a model assigns to a particular prediction. It indicates how confident the model is in its prediction for a given input.

In binary classification tasks, the confidence score typically represents the probability that the given instance belongs to the positive class (class 1). For example, if the confidence score for a prediction is 0.8, it means that the model is 80% confident that the instance belongs to the positive class.

In multiclass classification tasks, the confidence score usually represents the probability distribution across all possible classes. Each class will have its own confidence score, and the sum of all confidence scores will be equal to 1. For example, if a model predicts the probabilities of three classes as 0.3, 0.5, and 0.2 respectively, it means the model is 30% confident the instance belongs to the first class, 50% confident it belongs to the second class, and 20% confident it belongs to the third class.

Confidence scores are crucial for assessing the reliability of model predictions. Higher confidence scores indicate stronger predictions, while lower confidence scores suggest uncertainty. In practical applications, decision thresholds can be set based on confidence scores to make decisions or take actions, such as classifying instances into different categories or triggering alerts.

Another popular approach to multiclass classification is the one-vs-one (OvO) strategy, where a binary classifier is trained for each pair of classes. In this approach, the class with the most votes among all binary classifiers is selected as the final predicted class. The OvO strategy is more computationally intensive than OvA, as it requires training multiple binary classifiers. However, it can be more accurate and robust, especially in scenarios with imbalanced class distributions or overlapping class boundaries.

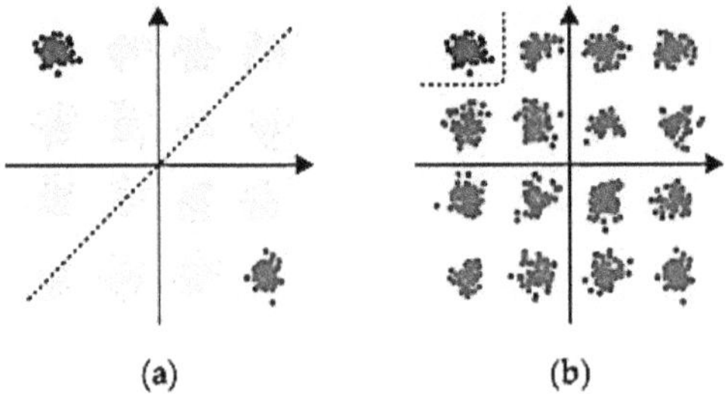

Figure 20: (a)One-vs-One (b) One-vs-All[17]

In addition to OvA and OvO, there are other multiclass classification techniques, such as multinomial logistic regression, multinomial naive Bayes, and multiclass support vector machines . These algorithms are specifically designed to handle multiclass classification tasks and may offer advantages in terms of accuracy, efficiency, or interpretability, depending on the characteristics of the dataset and the complexity of the problem.

---

[17] Image Source : https://www.researchgate.net/profile/Stephan-Pachnicke/publication/335739578/figure/fig2/AS:801851398176779@1568187679950/Illustration-of-one-iteration-during-training-for-a-OVO-b-OVA-and-c-BCSVM-methods_W640.jpg

Example

Classifying images of animals into different categories such as "dog," "cat," "bird," and "fish." Here's how the process might work:

1. **Data Collection:** Gather a dataset of labeled images of animals. Each image should be labeled with its corresponding class (e.g., "dog," "cat," "bird," or "fish").

2. **Data Preprocessing:** Preprocess the images to ensure they are all of the same size, format, and quality. Additionally, you may apply techniques such as normalization or data augmentation to improve model performance.

3. **Feature Extraction:** Extract meaningful features from the images that can be used for classification. This step may involve techniques like extracting color histograms, edge detection, or using pre-trained convolutional neural network (CNN) models to extract features.

4. **Model Training:** Train a multiclass classification model using a suitable algorithm such as a CNN. The model will take the extracted features of the images as input and learn to predict the correct class label for each image.

5. **Evaluation:** Evaluate the performance of the trained model using a separate validation dataset. Metrics such as accuracy,

precision, recall, and F1-score can be used to assess how well the model is performing across all classes.

6. **Prediction:** Once the model is trained and evaluated, it can be used to classify new, unseen images of animals into one of the predefined classes. The model will output a probability distribution over all classes, and the class with the highest probability can be selected as the predicted class for the image.

7. **Deployment:** Deploy the trained model in a real-world application where it can classify images of animals into different categories automatically.

This example illustrates how multiclass classification can be applied to the task of identifying and categorizing images of animals into multiple classes. Similar approaches can be used for various other multiclass classification tasks in different domains such as text classification, speech recognition, or medical diagnosis.

Accuracy: Accuracy is a measure of the overall correctness of a classification model. It is calculated as the ratio of the number of correctly predicted instances to the total number of instances in the dataset. Mathematically, accuracy is defined as:

Accuracy = Number of Correct Predictions/Total Number of Predictions

Accuracy provides an overall assessment of how well a model is performing across all classes.

Precision: Precision is a measure of the correctness of positive predictions made by a classification model. It is calculated as the ratio of the number of true positive predictions to the total number of positive predictions (true positives and false positives). Mathematically, precision is defined as:

Precision = True Positives/(True Positives + False Positives)

Precision is particularly useful when the cost of false positives is high.

Recall: Recall, also known as sensitivity or true positive rate, is a measure of the completeness of positive predictions made by a classification model. It is calculated as the ratio of the number of true positive predictions to the total number of actual positive instances (true positives and false negatives). Mathematically, recall is defined as:

Recall = True Positives/(True Positives + False Negatives)

Recall is particularly useful when the cost of false negatives is high.

F1-score: The F1-score is the harmonic mean of precision and recall. It provides a balanced measure of a model's performance by considering both precision and recall. The F1-score is calculated as:

F1-score = 2 × (Precision × Recall) / (Precision + Recall)

The F1-score ranges from 0 to 1, where a higher value indicates better model performance. It is especially useful when there is an uneven class distribution in the dataset.

These metrics are commonly used to evaluate the performance of classification models and provide insights into their strengths and weaknesses.

Overall, multiclass classifiers are essential tools in NLP for handling tasks with multiple classes or categories. By leveraging these algorithms, NLP systems can effectively classify text data into diverse categories, enabling a wide range of language processing applications and facilitating the analysis and interpretation of textual information.

------------------- *End of chapter 4* -------------------

5 Deep Learning for NLP

In the last few years, Deep Learning has become really important in NLP. It's changed how machines understand, create, and work with human language. In this chapter, we'll learn about Deep Learning for NLP. We'll look at how neural networks are used to solve language tasks. From things like word embeddings and recurrent neural networks to more advanced models like transformers, Deep Learning gives us lots of ways to teach machines to understand language better than ever before.

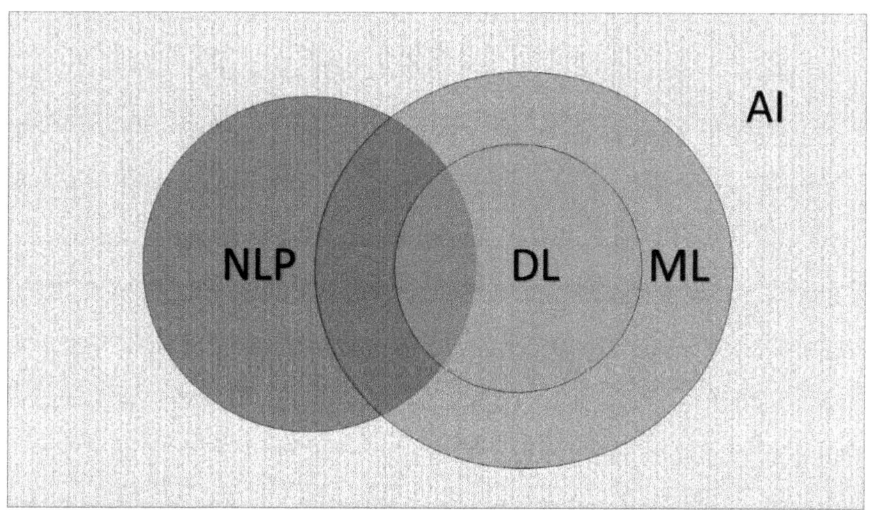

Figure 21: DL-ML-NLP-AI all connected with each other

Deep Learning leverages neural networks with multiple layers to automatically learn hierarchical representations of data, enabling machines to capture intricate relationships and nuances in textual data. In NLP, Deep Learning has achieved remarkable success in various tasks, including language modelling, sentiment analysis, machine translation, question answering, and text generation. By learning from large amounts of text data, deep neural networks can extract meaningful features, learn semantic representations, and generate human-like responses, pushing the boundaries of what machines can achieve in understanding and processing language.

Throughout this chapter, we will delve into the foundational concepts of Deep Learning for NLP, including neural network architectures, training techniques, and evaluation methodologies. We will explore popular deep learning models such as convolutional neural networks (CNNs), recurrent neural networks (RNNs), long short-term memory networks (LSTMs), and transformer architectures, discussing their strengths, weaknesses, and practical applications in NLP tasks. By gaining a deeper understanding of Deep Learning techniques in NLP, readers will be equipped with the knowledge and skills to leverage these advanced methodologies to solve complex language processing challenges and drive innovation in the field.

5.1 Introduction to Neural Networks

Neural networks form the foundation of Deep Learning, offering a powerful framework for modelling complex relationships and patterns in data. Inspired by the structure and function of the human brain, neural networks consist of interconnected nodes (neurons) organized into layers, each performing simple computational tasks. In NLP, neural networks have revolutionized the way machines understand and process human language, enabling the development of sophisticated language models capable of capturing semantic representations and generating context-aware responses.

The basic building block of a neural network is the artificial neuron, which takes input signals, applies weights to them, and passes the weighted sum through an activation function to produce an output. By connecting neurons in layers and stacking multiple layers together, neural networks can learn hierarchical representations of data, capturing increasingly abstract features at each layer.

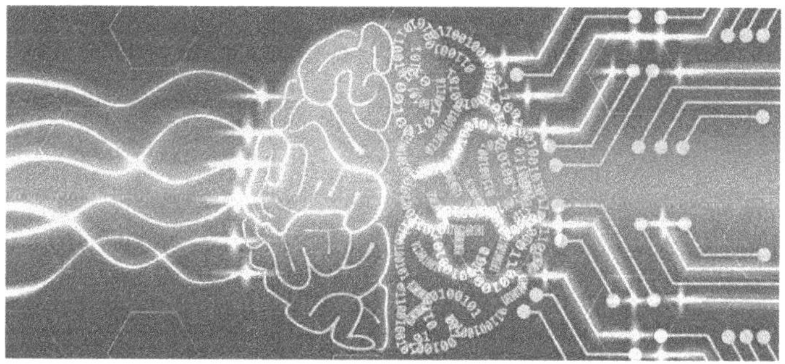

Figure 22: Human brain network vs. Artificial neural network[18]

[18] Image Source : https://home.sophos.com/sites/default/files/2021-09/ai-article-pic8.jpeg

In NLP, neural networks are often used to learn distributed representations of words (word embeddings), model sequential dependencies in text (recurrent neural networks), and process variable-length sequences of data (sequence-to-sequence models).

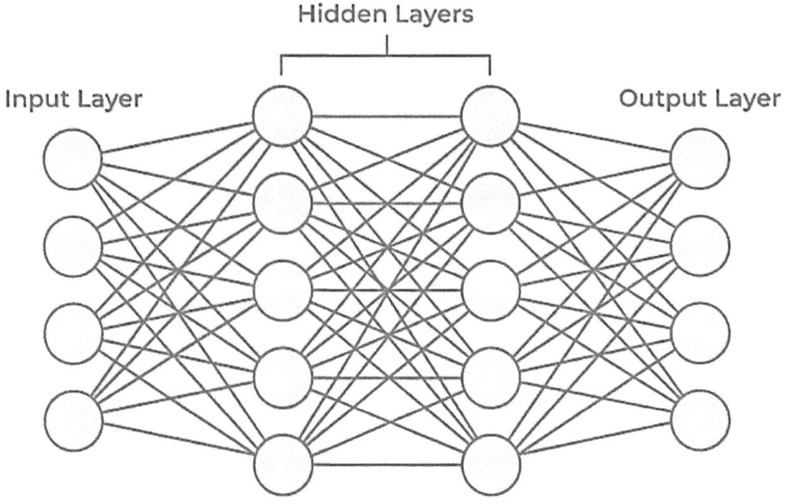

Figure 23: Artificial Neural Network Layers[19]

One of the key advantages of neural networks in NLP is their ability to automatically learn from large amounts of text data, without the need for manual feature engineering. Through the process of backpropagation and gradient descent, neural networks can

[19] Image Source : https://media.geeksforgeeks.org/wp-content/cdn-uploads/20230602113310/Neural-Networks-Architecture.png

iteratively adjust their weights to minimize prediction errors and optimize performance on language tasks. This data-driven approach enables neural networks to learn intricate patterns and nuances in language, leading to state-of-the-art performance in tasks such as language modelling, sentiment analysis, machine translation, and text generation.

Feature engineering is the process of selecting, creating, or transforming features (input variables) in a dataset to improve the performance of machine learning models. It's a crucial step in the machine learning pipeline because the quality and relevance of features greatly impact the model's ability to learn and generalize from the data.

5.2 Recurrent Neural Networks and Long Short-Term Memory Networks

Recurrent Neural Networks (RNNs) and Long Short-Term Memory (LSTM) networks arc powerful architectures in the domain of sequence modelling and processing, particularly in NLP. Unlike traditional feedforward neural networks, RNNs and LSTMs can effectively capture sequential dependencies and temporal dynamics in sequential data, making them well-suited for tasks involving sequences of varying lengths, such as text data.

Let's say we have the following sentence: "The movie was fantastic, but the ending was disappointing."

To perform sentiment analysis using a recurrent neural network (RNN) or a Long Short-Term Memory (LSTM) network, we can represent each word in the sentence as a vector using techniques like word embeddings (e.g., Word2Vec, GloVe). Then, we feed these word vectors sequentially into the RNN or LSTM model.

As the model processes each word vector, it updates its hidden state based on the information from previous words. This allows the model to capture the contextual information and sequential dependencies within the sentence. For example, when the model encounters the word "fantastic," it might start leaning towards a positive sentiment, but when it encounters "disappointing" later in the sentence, it can adjust its prediction accordingly.

Finally, the output of the RNN or LSTM can be passed through a *softmax* layer to obtain the probability distribution over the sentiment classes (positive, negative, neutral), and the class with the highest probability can be selected as the predicted sentiment for the input sentence.

This demonstrates how RNNs and LSTMs can effectively capture the sequential nature of text data and perform sentiment analysis by considering the context and dependencies between words in a sentence.

RNNs are designed to process sequential data by maintaining hidden states that capture information from previous time steps and propagate it to subsequent time steps. This recurrent nature allows RNNs to model long-range dependencies and context in sequences, making them suitable for tasks such as language modelling, part-of-speech tagging, and machine translation. However, standard RNNs suffer from the vanishing gradient problem, where gradients diminish exponentially over time, limiting their ability to capture long-range dependencies effectively.

To address the limitations of standard RNNs, LSTM networks were introduced, featuring a more complex architecture with specialized memory cells that can retain information over long periods. LSTM networks include three gates—input, forget, and output gates—that regulate the flow of information, allowing the network to selectively update and forget information based on the input sequence. This gating mechanism enables LSTMs to learn long-term dependencies and mitigate the vanishing gradient problem, making them particularly effective for tasks that require modelling complex sequential patterns, such as sentiment analysis, named entity recognition, and text generation.

In NLP, RNNs and LSTMs have been successfully applied to a wide range of tasks, including language modelling, machine translation, sentiment analysis, and speech recognition. Their ability to model sequential data and capture contextual information has led to significant advancements in language understanding and generation. However, RNNs and LSTMs have limitations, such as difficulty in capturing very long-term dependencies and computational inefficiency, which have motivated the development of more advanced architectures, such as transformer models.

5.3 Convolutional Neural Networks

Convolutional Neural Networks (CNNs) have emerged as powerful tools in for tasks involving sequential data such as text. Originally developed for image processing, CNNs have been adapted to NLP by treating text data as one-dimensional signals. One of the key strengths of CNNs lies in their ability to automatically learn hierarchical representations of features from raw input data. In the context of NLP, CNNs can effectively capture local patterns and dependencies within text, making them particularly suitable for tasks such as text classification, sentiment analysis, and named entity recognition.

At the heart of CNNs are convolutional layers, which apply convolutional filters across input data to extract local features. These filters slide across the input text, capturing patterns such as word combinations, phrases, and syntactic structures. By stacking multiple convolutional layers with non-linear activation functions such as ReLU (Rectified Linear Unit), CNNs can learn increasingly complex and abstract representations of text data. Additionally, pooling layers are often used to downsample the feature maps generated by convolutional layers, reducing the dimensionality of the data while preserving important information.

ReLU, or Rectified Linear Unit, is an activation function commonly used in neural networks. It is defined as:

ReLU(x)=max(0,x)

This means that it outputs the input directly if it is positive; otherwise, it outputs zero. ReLU is favored for its simplicity and effectiveness, offering computational efficiency and helping to mitigate the vanishing gradient problem, thus facilitating the training of deep networks. Variants like Leaky ReLU and Parametric ReLU address specific limitations of the standard ReLU function.

CNNs have demonstrated impressive performance in a wide range of NLP tasks, achieving state-of-the-art results on benchmark datasets. Their ability to automatically learn hierarchical representations of text data, combined with their computational efficiency and scalability, has made them a popular choice for NLP practitioners. Moreover, CNNs can be easily integrated with other deep learning architectures such as RNNs and transformer models, further enhancing their capabilities. Overall, CNNs represent a versatile and effective tool for processing text data in NLP, enabling researchers and practitioners to tackle a variety of language understanding and generation tasks with remarkable success.

5.4 Sequence-to-Sequence Models

Sequence-to-Sequence (Seq2Seq) models have revolutionized many NLP tasks by providing a framework for processing variable-length input sequences and generating corresponding output sequences. Originally popularized for machine translation tasks, Seq2Seq models have since been applied to a wide range of tasks such as text summarization, dialogue generation, and question answering. At the core of Seq2Seq models is an encoder-decoder architecture, where an encoder network processes the input sequence and generates a fixed-length representation, which is then fed into a decoder network to generate the output sequence.

The encoder network of a Seq2Seq model typically consists of RNN layers or transformer encoders, which process the input sequence one token at a time and generate a context vector representing the entire input sequence. This context vector captures the salient information from the input sequence and serves as the initial state for the decoder network. The decoder network, on the other hand, is responsible for generating the output sequence based on the context vector generated by the encoder. It uses another set of RNN layers or transformer decoders to generate tokens sequentially, conditioning on the context vector and previously generated tokens.

Seq2Seq models have proven to be highly effective for tasks that involve mapping variable-length input sequences to variable-length output sequences. They excel at tasks such as machine translation, where the input and output sequences have different lengths and require capturing complex dependencies between words. Additionally, Seq2Seq models have been successfully applied to tasks such as text summarization, where the goal is to generate a concise summary of a longer document, and dialogue generation, where the model generates natural-sounding responses in conversation settings. Overall, Seq2Seq models represent a powerful framework for tackling a wide range of sequence-to-sequence tasks in NLP, offering flexibility, scalability, and state-of-the-art performance in various applications.

5.5 Transfer Learning

Transfer learning has emerged as a powerful technique in Natural Language Processing that leverages pretrained models to improve the performance of downstream tasks with limited labeled data. The basic idea behind transfer learning is to train a model on a large dataset and then transfer the knowledge learned from that dataset to a related but different task. In the context of NLP, transfer learning often involves using pretrained language models that have been trained on large corpora of text data using unsupervised learning objectives such as language modeling or masked language modeling.

One of the key benefits of transfer learning in NLP is its ability to overcome the limitations of traditional machine learning approaches that require large amounts of annotated data for training. By pretraining a language model on a large corpus of text data, the model learns rich representations of language that capture syntactic, semantic, and contextual information. These representations can then be fine-tuned on a smaller labeled dataset for the specific downstream task, allowing the model to adapt to the nuances of the task while retaining the knowledge learned during pretraining.

Transfer learning has been widely adopted in NLP and has led to significant improvements in various downstream tasks, including text classification, sentiment analysis, named entity recognition, and machine translation. Pretrained language models such as BERT, GPT, and XLNet have achieved state-of-the-art performance on benchmark datasets across a wide range of tasks, demonstrating the effectiveness of transfer learning in NLP. Moreover, transfer learning has enabled researchers and practitioners to build more robust and accurate NLP systems with less labeled data, making it a valuable tool for advancing the state of the art in the field.

5.6 Evaluation Metrics

Evaluation metrics play a crucial role in assessing the performance of Natural Language Processing models and systems across various tasks. These metrics provide quantitative measures of how well a model performs on a specific task, helping to compare different models, fine-tune parameters, and track progress over time. In NLP, several evaluation metrics are commonly used, each tailored to the specific characteristics of the task at hand.

For classification tasks such as text classification, sentiment analysis, and named entity recognition, common evaluation metrics include accuracy, precision, recall, and F1 score. Accuracy measures the proportion of correctly classified instances, while precision measures the proportion of true positive instances among all instances classified as positive, and recall measures the proportion of true positive instances that are correctly classified. The F1 score is the harmonic mean of precision and recall, providing a balanced measure of a model's performance.

In tasks such as machine translation, text summarization, and question answering, evaluation metrics such as BLEU score, ROUGE score, and METEOR score are commonly used. BLEU (Bilingual Evaluation Understudy) score measures the overlap between the generated output and reference translations based on n-gram precision, while ROUGE (Recall-Oriented Understudy for Gisting Evaluation) score measures the overlap between generated summaries and reference summaries based on n-gram recall. METEOR (Metric for Evaluation of Translation with Explicit Ordering) score is a more comprehensive metric that considers both n-gram overlap and semantic similarity between generated and reference translations.

Overall, the choice of evaluation metrics depends on the specific NLP task and the characteristics of the data. By using appropriate evaluation metrics, researchers and practitioners can accurately assess the performance of NLP models and systems, identify areas for improvement, and make informed decisions about model selection and optimization.

5.7 Applications of Deep Learning in NLP

Deep learning has revolutionized various aspects of Natural Language Processing by offering powerful tools and techniques to solve complex language-related tasks. One of the primary applications of deep learning in NLP is text classification, where models learn to categorize text documents into predefined categories or labels. This has found widespread use in sentiment analysis, spam detection, topic classification, and more. Deep learning models, such as Convolutional Neural Networks and Recurrent Neural

Networks, have demonstrated superior performance in capturing intricate patterns in text data, enabling accurate classification across different domains.

Another significant application of deep learning in NLP is language generation, where models learn to generate human-like text based on given prompts or contexts. This includes tasks such as machine translation, text summarization, dialogue generation, and story generation. Advanced architectures like Transformer-based models, such as BERT and GPT, have achieved remarkable success in these tasks by leveraging large-scale pretraining on vast text corpora. These models can understand and generate coherent and contextually relevant text, making them valuable tools for various applications, including content generation, conversational agents, and content summarization.

GPT stands for Generative Pre-trained Transformer.

Generative: Refers to the model's ability to generate text.

Pre-trained: Indicates that the model is pre-trained on a large corpus of text before being fine-tuned for specific tasks.

Transformer: Refers to the type of neural network architecture used, which is particularly effective for natural language processing tasks.

Deep learning has also been extensively applied in information retrieval and extraction tasks, such as named entity recognition, entity linking, and question answering. Models trained on large text corpora can effectively extract relevant information from unstructured text data, enabling tasks like named entity recognition to identify entities such as names of people, organizations, and locations. Additionally, deep learning models have been used in question answering systems to understand and generate responses to user queries by extracting relevant information from text sources. Overall, deep learning has paved the way for significant advancements in NLP, enabling a wide range of applications that facilitate language understanding, generation, and interaction in various domains.

5.8 Challenges and Future Direction

Despite the remarkable advancements made in recent years, Natural Language Processing still faces several challenges that pave the way for future research directions. One significant challenge is the development of models that can understand and generate text with a deeper understanding of context and semantics. While current models, such as transformer-based architectures like BERT and GPT, have made impressive strides in this direction, there is still room for improvement in capturing nuanced meanings, context shifts, and commonsense reasoning in text data.

Another challenge in NLP is the development of models that can generalize well across diverse domains and languages. Many existing models are trained on large corpora of text data in specific domains or languages, leading to biases and limitations in their generalizability. Future research should focus on developing more robust and adaptable models that can transfer knowledge across domains and languages, enabling applications in diverse real-world scenarios.

Ethical and societal considerations also pose challenges in the field of NLP. Issues such as bias in data and models, fairness, transparency, and privacy concerns need to be addressed to ensure that NLP technologies are developed and deployed responsibly. Researchers and practitioners must actively work towards developing unbiased and inclusive models and frameworks that prioritize fairness and equity in language processing tasks.

Looking ahead, future research directions in NLP are likely to focus on addressing these challenges and advancing the state-of-the-art in various domains. This includes exploring novel architectures and algorithms, incorporating multimodal information (such as text, images, and audio), enhancing interpretability and explainability of models, and developing more efficient and scalable techniques for training and deploying NLP systems.

By tackling these challenges and exploring new frontiers, the field of NLP is poised to continue its rapid evolution and make significant contributions to language understanding, generation, and interaction in the years to come.

------------------- *End of chapter 5* -------------------

6 Practical Applications

The chapter on practical applications of Natural Language Processing delves into the real-world use cases and implementations of NLP technologies across various industries and domains. As NLP continues to evolve and mature, its practical applications have become increasingly diverse and impactful, ranging from customer service automation and sentiment analysis to healthcare informatics and financial analytics. This chapter aims to provide readers with insights into how NLP techniques and tools are being deployed in practical settings to address complex challenges and unlock new opportunities.

In this chapter, we will explore a wide range of practical applications of NLP, showcasing examples from different industries and sectors. From improving customer experience and enhancing business intelligence to advancing healthcare outcomes and facilitating communication, NLP technologies are driving innovation and transformation in numerous fields. Through case studies, examples, and best practices, this chapter will demonstrate how organizations are leveraging NLP to extract valuable insights from unstructured text data, automate repetitive tasks, and augment human capabilities in decision-making and problem-solving.

Whether you are a practitioner seeking to understand how NLP can be applied in your domain or an enthusiast curious about the real-world impact of NLP technologies, this chapter will provide valuable insights and inspiration. By examining practical applications and success stories, we aim to showcase the immense potential of NLP to revolutionize industries, improve efficiency, and empower individuals and organizations to achieve their goals. Join us on a journey through the practical applications of NLP and discover the transformative power of language processing technologies in action.

6.1 Sentiment analysis

Sentiment analysis, also known as opinion mining, is a powerful NLP technique used to analyze and categorize text data based on the sentiment expressed within the text. It involves determining whether a piece of text expresses positive, negative, or neutral sentiment towards a particular topic or entity. Sentiment analysis has numerous real-world applications across various industries, including marketing, customer service, social media monitoring, and market research. In this section, we will delve into the details of sentiment analysis, including its methodologies, applications, and real-world examples.

6.1.1 Methodologies of Sentiment analysis

1. Lexicon-based Sentiment Analysis:

- Lexicon-based approaches use sentiment lexicons or dictionaries containing lists of words and their associated sentiment scores.
- Words are assigned sentiment scores (e.g., positive, negative, neutral) based on their presence in the lexicon.
- The sentiment score of a piece of text is computed by aggregating the sentiment scores of individual words.

2. Machine Learning-based Sentiment Analysis:

- Machine learning approaches involve training supervised or unsupervised models on labeled datasets of text data.
- Supervised models, such as Support Vector Machines, Naive Bayes, and Neural Networks, are trained on annotated text data with sentiment labels.
- Unsupervised models, such as K-means clustering and Latent Dirichlet Allocation, learn sentiment patterns from unlabeled text data.

3. Deep Learning-based Sentiment Analysis:

- Deep learning models, such as Convolutional Neural Networks and Recurrent Neural Networks, have been applied to sentiment analysis tasks.
- Models like Long Short-Term Memory networks and Transformer-based architectures (e.g., BERT) have achieved state-of-the-art performance in sentiment analysis by capturing complex linguistic patterns and contextual information.

6.1.2 Applications of Sentiment analysis

6.1.2.1 Customer Feedback Analysis

- Companies use sentiment analysis to analyze customer feedback from various sources, such as surveys, reviews, and social media posts.

- By understanding customer sentiment, businesses can identify areas for improvement, address customer concerns, and enhance customer satisfaction.

6.1.2.2 Brand Monitoring and Reputation Management

- Sentiment analysis is used to monitor online conversations and social media mentions related to a brand or product.

- Companies track sentiment trends to gauge public perception, identify brand advocates and detractors, and manage reputation risks.

6.1.2.3 Market Research and Competitive Analysis

- Market researchers use sentiment analysis to analyze consumer sentiment towards products, brands, and advertising campaigns.

- By monitoring sentiment trends and analyzing competitor mentions, companies can gain insights into market dynamics, consumer preferences, and emerging trends.

Conclusion

Sentiment analysis is a valuable tool for extracting insights from text data and understanding public opinion, customer sentiment, and market trends. By employing various methodologies and leveraging advanced NLP techniques, organizations can gain actionable insights from text data, drive informed decision-making, and enhance customer experiences. As sentiment analysis continues to evolve, it will play an increasingly important role in shaping business strategies, driving innovation, and improving outcomes across industries.

6.2 Classifications

6.2.1 Text classification

Text classification, also known as text categorization, is the process of assigning predefined categories or labels to text documents based on their content. It is a fundamental task in Natural Language Processing and has numerous real-world applications, including sentiment analysis, spam detection, topic classification, and language identification.

6.2.2 Binary Classification

Binary classification is a type of text classification where documents are categorized into one of two classes or categories. For example, in sentiment analysis, documents may be classified as either positive or negative based on the sentiment expressed in the text. Another example is spam detection, where emails are classified as either spam or not spam.

Example: Sentiment Analysis of Movie Reviews

Task: Classifying movie reviews as either positive or negative based on the sentiment expressed in the text.

Dataset: Dataset with movie reviews labeled as positive or negative.

Approach: Train a machine learning model (e.g., Support Vector Machine or Naive Bayes classifier) on labeled movie reviews data.

Evaluation: Evaluate the model's performance using metrics like accuracy, precision, recall, and F1 score.

6.2.3 Topic Classification

Topic classification, also known as topic modeling or document classification, involves categorizing text documents into predefined topics or themes. Each document is assigned to one or more topics based on the main subject or content covered in the text. Topic classification is widely used in news categorization, document organization, and content recommendation systems.

Example: News Categorization

Task: Categorizing news articles into topics such as politics, sports, entertainment, technology, etc.

Dataset: A collection of news articles from various sources labeled with their corresponding topics.

Approach: Train a machine learning model or utilize unsupervised topic modeling techniques (e.g., Latent Dirichlet Allocation) to identify topics in the text data.

Evaluation: Assess the model's performance using metrics like accuracy or coherence score for topic modeling approaches.

6.2.4 Multiclass Classification

Multiclass classification involves categorizing text documents into more than two classes or categories. Each document can belong to one and only one class out of multiple possible classes. Multiclass classification tasks include topic classification with multiple topics, language identification, and document tagging.

Example: Language Identification

Task: Identifying the language of text documents from a set of predefined languages (e.g., English, Spanish, French, German, etc.).

Dataset: Text documents written in different languages, labeled with their corresponding languages.

Approach: Train a machine learning model or utilize language identification libraries (e.g., LangDetect) to classify text documents into predefined languages.

Evaluation: Measure the model's accuracy and performance on correctly identifying the language of text documents.

Conclusion

Text classification is a fundamental task in NLP with diverse applications in various domains. Whether it's binary classification for sentiment analysis, topic classification for news categorization, or multiclass classification for language identification, text classification techniques enable automated analysis and organization of textual data, facilitating decision-making and information retrieval processes in real-world scenarios.

6.2.5 Named Entity Recognition

NER algorithms analyze the tokenized text and identify spans of words that constitute named entities.

The identified entities are classified into predefined categories, such as person names, organization names, etc.

NER models may utilize various techniques, including rule-based approaches, machine learning algorithms (e.g., Conditional Random Fields, Recurrent Neural Networks), and deep learning architectures (e.g., Transformer-based models like BERT).

Example

Consider the following sentence: "Apple Inc. is headquartered in Cupertino, California, and was founded by Steve Jobs, Steve Wozniak, and Ronald Wayne."

NER would identify and classify the following named entities:

Organization: "Apple Inc."
Location: "Cupertino, California"
Person: "Steve Jobs", "Steve Wozniak", "Ronald Wayne"

6.2.5.1 Applications of Named Entity Recognition

1. Information Extraction: NER is used to extract structured information from unstructured text data, facilitating tasks such as building knowledge graphs, entity linking, and semantic search.
2. Document Summarization: Named entities play a crucial role in document summarization by identifying key entities and events mentioned in the text.
3. Question Answering: NER helps identify relevant entities mentioned in questions and corresponding answers, improving the accuracy of question answering systems.
4. Information Retrieval: Named entities serve as important features for indexing and retrieving documents in information retrieval systems.

6.2.5.2 Challenges in Named Entity Recognition

1. Ambiguity: Named entities may have multiple interpretations or contexts, leading to ambiguity in classification.
2. Variability: Named entities may vary in their representations and formats across different texts and domains.
3. Out-of-Vocabulary Entities: NER models may struggle to recognize named entities that are rare or unseen in the training data.

Conclusion

Named Entity Recognition is a critical task in NLP for identifying and classifying named entities within text data. By accurately extracting and categorizing entities, NER enables a wide range of downstream applications, including information extraction, document summarization, question answering, and information retrieval. Despite its challenges, ongoing advancements in NER algorithms and techniques continue to improve the accuracy and robustness of named entity recognition systems, making them invaluable tools for extracting structured knowledge from unstructured text data.

------------------- *End of chapter 6* -------------------

7 Ethical Considerations in NLP

The chapter on ethical considerations in Natural Language Processing discusses complex and nuanced ethical challenges. These challenges come with developing, deploying, and using NLP technologies. As NLP continues to advance, it affects many parts of our lives. It is important to look closely at the ethical implications of these technologies. We need to ensure that NLP is developed and used in a responsible and ethical way. This chapter explores the ethical aspects of NLP. It aims to raise awareness about potential risks and biases. It also provides guidance on ethical best practices for researchers, practitioners, and policymakers.

In this chapter, we will address a range of ethical considerations in NLP, including issues related to fairness, transparency, accountability, privacy, and bias. We will examine how NLP technologies can inadvertently perpetuate existing societal biases, reinforce stereotypes, and infringe upon individuals' privacy and rights. Through case studies, examples, and discussions, we will explore the ethical dilemmas faced by NLP researchers and practitioners and highlight the importance of ethical awareness and responsibility in the development and deployment of NLP systems.

Whether you are a researcher, developer, policymaker, or end-user of NLP technologies, this chapter will provide valuable insights into the ethical dimensions of NLP and empower you to navigate the ethical challenges inherent in this rapidly evolving field. By promoting ethical awareness, fostering dialogue, and advocating for ethical best practices, we can work together to ensure that NLP technologies serve the greater good and uphold principles of fairness, justice, and respect for human dignity. Join us on a journey through the ethical considerations in NLP and discover how we can harness the power of language processing technologies for positive societal impact while mitigating potential risks and harms.

7.1 Bias and fairness in NLP algorithms

Bias and fairness in NLP algorithms are important topics. They need careful consideration and scrutiny. NLP algorithms, like any other machine learning models, can have biases. These biases come from the data they are trained on and the model development process. For example, if an NLP model is trained on data that mostly represents one gender, it might favor that gender. This can lead to biased outcomes in applications like job applicant screening or performance reviews.

Another example is cultural stereotypes. If an NLP model is trained on text that includes cultural stereotypes, it might reinforce these stereotypes. For instance, a translation system might translate job titles in a gender-biased way, such as translating "doctor" to a male equivalent and "nurse" to a female equivalent.

Systemic inequalities can also be a source of bias. If the training data reflects societal inequalities, the NLP model can learn and perpetuate these inequalities. For example, predictive policing algorithms might unfairly target certain communities based on biased historical data.

These biases can lead to unfair outcomes and discriminatory practices. It is important to identify and mitigate these biases to ensure fairness in NLP systems.

One of the key challenges in addressing bias and fairness in NLP algorithms is the lack of diverse and representative training data. Training data often reflects existing societal biases and inequalities, which can result in biased model predictions and discriminatory behaviour. For example, NLP models trained on biased text corpora may exhibit racial, gender, or socio-economic biases in their language processing capabilities, leading to disparities in performance across different demographic groups.

To mitigate bias and promote fairness in NLP algorithms, researchers and practitioners have proposed various approaches and techniques. These include data augmentation to diversify training data, debiasing algorithms to mitigate unwanted biases, and fairness-aware learning methods to ensure equitable outcomes. Additionally, transparency and interpretability measures such as model explainability and fairness metrics play a crucial role in identifying and mitigating biases in NLP systems.

Addressing bias and fairness in NLP algorithms require a multi-faceted approach that involves collaboration between researchers, developers, policymakers, and end-users. It requires ongoing efforts to collect diverse and representative training data, develop bias-aware algorithms, and establish ethical guidelines and standards for NLP research and development. By proactively addressing bias and fairness concerns, we can build NLP systems that are more equitable, inclusive, and respectful of human diversity, ultimately fostering trust and confidence in these transformative technologies.

7.2 Privacy concerns and data protection

Privacy concerns and data protection arc paramount in the field of Natural Language Processing, given the sensitive nature of textual data and the potential risks associated with its processing. NLP algorithms often require access to large volumes of text data, which may include personal information, confidential communications, and other sensitive content. As such, ensuring the privacy and protection of individuals' data is essential to uphold their rights and maintain trust in NLP technologies.

One of the primary privacy concerns in NLP is the risk of inadvertent disclosure of sensitive information through text processing. NLP models may inadvertently reveal personal details, medical information, financial data, or other confidential content contained within text documents. Additionally, the aggregation and analysis of large-scale text data may lead to the identification of individuals, even when data has been anonymized or pseudonymized. These privacy risks highlight the need for robust data anonymization techniques, encryption protocols, and access controls to safeguard sensitive text data from unauthorized access or disclosure.

Furthermore, the proliferation of NLP technologies, such as language models and chatbots, raises concerns about user privacy and data security. These systems often interact with users in real-time, processing their text inputs and generating responses based on learned patterns and contexts. However, this interaction may involve the collection and storage of personal data, posing privacy risks if not handled appropriately. Ensuring transparent data handling practices, obtaining informed consent from users, and implementing privacy-preserving technologies, such as differential privacy and federated learning, are essential steps to mitigate these risks and protect user privacy.

In addition to individual privacy concerns, data protection regulations, such as the General Data Protection Regulation (GDPR) in Europe and the California Consumer Privacy Act (CCPA) in the United States, impose legal obligations on organizations that collect, process, or store text data. These regulations require organizations to implement appropriate technical and organizational measures to ensure the privacy, security, and lawful processing of personal data, including textual information. Compliance with these regulations necessitates the adoption of privacy-enhancing technologies, data governance frameworks, and robust data protection practices throughout the NLP lifecycle.

In conclusion, privacy concerns and data protection are integral aspects of NLP research, development, and deployment. By prioritizing privacy-by-design principles, adopting privacy-preserving technologies, and adhering to data protection regulations, we can build NLP systems that respect individuals' privacy rights, uphold ethical standards, and foster trust and confidence in the responsible use of textual data.

------------------- *End of chapter 7* -------------------

8 Handson Practice

In this chapter, we will walk through a complete NLP project. We'll start with a simple problem statement and guide you through the entire NLP pipeline step by step with the help of *python* programming language. By the end of this chapter, you'll have a solid understanding of how to implement an NLP solution from scratch.

8.1 Text preprocessing on string

```
import nltk
import pandas as pd
import string
from nltk.tokenize import word_tokenize
from nltk.corpus import stopwords
from nltk.stem import WordNetLemmatizer

# Download necessary NLTK data files
nltk.download('punkt')
nltk.download('stopwords')
nltk.download('wordnet')
nltk.download('omw-1.4')
```

```
# Step 2: Loading the Dataset
data = {
    'text': [
        "NLP is a field of artificial
intelligence!",
        "It's amazing how computers can
understand human language.",
        "Preprocessing text data is a crucial
step in NLP."
    ]
}

df = pd.DataFrame(data)
print("Original Data:")
print(df)

# Step 3: Tokenization
df['tokenized'] = df['text'].apply(word_tokenize)
print("\nTokenized Data:")
print(df[['text', 'tokenized']])

# Step 4: Lowercasing
df['lowercased'] = df['tokenized'].apply(lambda
x: [word.lower() for word in x])
```

```
print("\nLowercased Data:")
print(df[['text', 'lowercased']])

# Step 5: Removing Punctuation
def remove_punctuation(tokens):
    return [word for word in tokens if
word.isalpha()]

df['no_punctuation'] =
df['lowercased'].apply(remove_punctuation)
print("\nData without Punctuation:")
print(df[['text', 'no_punctuation']])

# Step 6: Removing Stopwords
stop_words = set(stopwords.words('english'))

def remove_stopwords(tokens):
    return [word for word in tokens if word not
in stop_words]

df['no_stopwords'] =
df['no_punctuation'].apply(remove_stopwords)
print("\nData without Stopwords:")
print(df[['text', 'no_stopwords']])
```

```
# Step 7: Lemmatization
lemmatizer = WordNetLemmatizer()

def lemmatize_tokens(tokens):
    return [lemmatizer.lemmatize(word) for word
in tokens]

df['lemmatized'] =
df['no_stopwords'].apply(lemmatize_tokens)
print("\nLemmatized Data:")
print(df[['text', 'lemmatized']])
```

Output

```
Original Data:
                                                 tex
t
0         NLP is a field of artificial intelligence
!
1  It's amazing how computers can understand huma..
.
2  Preprocessing text data is a crucial step in NLP
.

Tokenized Data:
                                                 tex
t  \
0         NLP is a field of artificial intelligence
!
1  It's amazing how computers can understand huma..
.
2  Preprocessing text data is a crucial step in NLP
.
```

```
                                              tokenize
d
0  [NLP, is, a, field, of, artificial, intelligen..
.
1  [It, 's, amazing, how, computers, can, underst..
.
2  [Preprocessing, text, data, is, a, crucial, st..
.

Lowercased Data:
                                                   tex
t  \
0         NLP is a field of artificial intelligence
!
1  It's amazing how computers can understand huma..
.
2  Preprocessing text data is a crucial step in NLP
.

                                             lowercase
d
0  [nlp, is, a, field, of, artificial, intelligen..
.
1  [it, 's, amazing, how, computers, can, underst..
.
2  [preprocessing, text, data, is, a, crucial, st..
.

Data without Punctuation:
                                                   tex
t  \
0         NLP is a field of artificial intelligence
!
1  It's amazing how computers can understand huma..
.
2  Preprocessing text data is a crucial step in NLP
.

                                        no_punctuatio
n
0  [nlp, is, a, field, of, artificial, intelligence
]
```

```
1  [it, amazing, how, computers, can, understand,..
.
2  [preprocessing, text, data, is, a, crucial, st..
.

Data without Stopwords:
                                                tex
t  \
0          NLP is a field of artificial intelligence
!
1  It's amazing how computers can understand huma..
.
2  Preprocessing text data is a crucial step in NLP
.

                                        no_stopword
s
0              [nlp, field, artificial, intelligence
]
1  [amazing, computers, understand, human, language
]
2    [preprocessing, text, data, crucial, step, nlp
]

Lemmatized Data:
                                                tex
t  \
0          NLP is a field of artificial intelligence
!
1  It's amazing how computers can understand huma..
.
2  Preprocessing text data is a crucial step in NLP
.

                                         lemmatized
0             [nlp, field, artificial, intelligence]
1  [amazing, computer, understand, human, language]
2   [preprocessing, text, data, crucial, step, nlp]
```

8.2 Spelling Correction and Normalization

```
import nltk
from nltk.tokenize import word_tokenize
from textblob import TextBlob
from nltk.stem import WordNetLemmatizer
from nltk.corpus import wordnet

# Download required NLTK data
nltk.download('punkt')
nltk.download('wordnet')
nltk.download('averaged_perceptron_tagger')

# Initial input
text = "Ths is an exmple of NLP txt preprocessing.
NLP helps in teh automted analysis of txt data."

# Tokenization
tokens = word_tokenize(text)

# Spelling Correction
corrected_tokens =
[str(TextBlob(token).correct()) for token in
tokens]
```

```
# Normalization
lemmatizer = WordNetLemmatizer()

def get_wordnet_pos(word):
    """Map POS tag to first character lemmatize()
accepts"""
    tag = nltk.pos_tag([word])[0][1][0].upper()
    tag_dict = {"J": wordnet.ADJ,
                "N": wordnet.NOUN,
                "V": wordnet.VERB,
                "R": wordnet.ADV}
    return tag_dict.get(tag, wordnet.NOUN)

normalized_tokens =
[lemmatizer.lemmatize(token.lower(),
get_wordnet_pos(token.lower())) for token in
corrected_tokens]

# Reconstructing the sentence
normalized_text = ' '.join(normalized_tokens)
print(normalized_text)
```

Output

```
the be an example of nlp txt preprocessing . nlp he
lp in the automted analysis of txt data .
```

8.3 Number extraction and NER on string

Console

```
pip install spacy
python -m spacy download en_core_web_sm
```

#Python Code

```
import re
import spacy

# Load the spaCy English model
nlp = spacy.load("en_core_web_sm")

def extract_numbers_and_ner(text):
    # Extract numbers using regular expressions
    numbers = re.findall(r'\d+', text)

    # Perform Named Entity Recognition (NER)
    doc = nlp(text)
    entities = [(ent.text, ent.label_) for ent in
doc.ents]

    return numbers, entities

# Example string
```

```
text = "John bought 12 apples and 5 oranges from
New York on June 5th, 2021."

# Extract numbers and named entities
numbers, entities = extract_numbers_and_ner(text)

print("Numbers:", numbers)
print("Named Entities:", entities)
```

Output

```
Numbers: ['12', '5', '5', '2021']
Named Entities: [('John', 'ORG'), ('12', 'CARDINAL'
), ('5', 'CARDINAL'), ('New York', 'GPE'), ('June 5
th, 2021', 'DATE')]
```

8.4 Binary classification of movie reviews

Let's work on a sentiment analysis task. Our goal is to classify movie reviews as positive or negative. We'll use a dataset of movie reviews from IMDb.

Step 1: Data Collection

We'll use the IMDb movie reviews dataset, which is available in many public repositories. For simplicity, we'll use a pre-downloaded version.

```
import pandas as pd
# Load dataset
data = pd.read_csv('imdb_movie_reviews.csv')
print(data.head())
```

Step 2: Data Preprocessing

Text data needs to be cleaned and preprocessed before it can be used for modeling.

```
import re
import nltk
from nltk.corpus import stopwords
nltk.download('stopwords')
stop_words = set(stopwords.words('english'))
def preprocess_text(text):
    # Remove HTML tags
    text = re.sub(r'<.*?>', '', text)
    # Remove non-alphabetic characters
    text = re.sub(r'[^a-zA-Z]', ' ', text)
    # Convert to lowercase
    text = text.lower()
    # Remove stopwords
    text = ' '.join([word for word in text.split()
if word not in stop_words])
    return text
```

```
data['cleaned_review']                                    =
data['review'].apply(preprocess_text)
print(data['cleaned_review'].head())
```

Step 3: Feature Extraction

Convert text data into numerical features using techniques like TF-IDF or word embeddings.

```
from sklearn.feature_extraction.text import
TfidfVectorizer
# Create TF-IDF features
vectorizer = TfidfVectorizer(max_features=5000)
X =
vectorizer.fit_transform(data['cleaned_review']).
toarray()
y = data['sentiment']
```

Step 4: Model Training

Train a machine learning model to classify the reviews

```
from sklearn.model_selection import
train_test_split
from sklearn.naive_bayes import MultinomialNB
from sklearn.metrics import accuracy_score,
classification_report
```

```
# Split data into training and testing sets
X_train, X_test, y_train, y_test =
train_test_split(X, y, test_size=0.2,
random_state=42)

# Train a Naive Bayes classifier
model = MultinomialNB()
model.fit(X_train, y_train)

# Make predictions
y_pred = model.predict(X_test)

# Evaluate the model
print(f'Accuracy: {accuracy_score(y_test,
y_pred)}')
print(classification_report(y_test, y_pred))
```

Step 5: Model Evaluation

Evaluate the model using appropriate metrics and visualize the results.

```
import matplotlib.pyplot as plt
import seaborn as sns
from sklearn.metrics import confusion_matrix
```

```
# Plot confusion matrix
conf_mat = confusion_matrix(y_test, y_pred)
sns.heatmap(conf_mat, annot=True, fmt='d',
cmap='Blues')
plt.xlabel('Predicted')
plt.ylabel('Actual')
plt.show()
```

Step 6: Model Deployment

Once the model is trained and evaluated, it's ready to be deployed for making predictions on new data.

```
def predict_sentiment(review):
    cleaned_review = preprocess_text(review)
    features                                        =
vectorizer.transform([cleaned_review]).toarray()
    prediction = model.predict(features)
    return  'Positive'  if  prediction  ==  1  else
'Negative'

# Test the deployment
new_review = "This movie was fantastic! I loved
it."
```

```
print(f'Review: {new_review}')
print(f'Sentiment:
{predict_sentiment(new_review)}')
```

8.5 Multiclass classification on set of words

Console

```
pip install scikit-learn
```

#Python Code

```
import numpy as np
from sklearn.tree import DecisionTreeClassifier
from sklearn.model_selection import
train_test_split
from sklearn.metrics import accuracy_score

# Sample words and their classes
words = ["apple", "banana", "grape", "kiwi",
"mango", "orange", "pear", "peach", "plum",
"strawberry"]
labels = ["medium", "long", "short", "short",
"short", "medium", "short", "short", "short",
"long"]
```

```
# Feature extraction function
def extract_features(word):
    length = len(word)
    vowels = sum(1 for char in word if char in
'aeiou')
    return [length, vowels]

# Convert words to features
X = np.array([extract_features(word) for word in
words])
# Convert labels to numerical format
label_map = {"short": 0, "medium": 1, "long": 2}
y = np.array([label_map[label] for label in
labels])

# Split the data into training and testing sets
X_train, X_test, y_train, y_test =
train_test_split(X, y, test_size=0.2,
random_state=42)

# Train the classifier
clf = DecisionTreeClassifier()
clf.fit(X_train, y_train)
```

```
# Make predictions
y_pred = clf.predict(X_test)

# Evaluate the classifier
accuracy = accuracy_score(y_test, y_pred)
print(f"Accuracy: {accuracy * 100:.2f}%")

# Function to predict the class of a new word
def predict_class(word):
    features = extract_features(word)
    prediction = clf.predict([features])
    class_map = {0: "short", 1: "medium", 2:
"long"}
    return class_map[prediction[0]]

# Example prediction
new_word = "blueberry"
predicted_class = predict_class(new_word)
print(f"The word '{new_word}' is classified as
'{predicted_class}'.")
```

Output

```
Accuracy: 50.00%
The word 'blueberry' is classified as 'medium'.
```

-------------------- *End of chapter 8* --------------------

9 NLP Practical Exercises

1. Tokenization: Write a function to split text into tokens (words or phrases).
2. Stopword Removal: Implement a function to remove stopwords from a text.
3. Stemming: Use a stemming algorithm (like Porter or Snowball) to reduce words to their root form.
4. Lemmatization: Implement lemmatization to reduce words to their base or dictionary form.
5. Part-of-Speech Tagging: Use a POS tagging library to label the parts of speech in a sentence.
6. Named Entity Recognition (NER): Use an NER library to identify and classify named entities in text.
7. Text Classification: Build a simple text classifier using Naive Bayes or SVM on labeled datasets.
8. Sentiment Analysis: Analyze the sentiment (positive, negative, neutral) of sentences or documents.
9. Word Frequency Analysis: Count the frequency of each word in a text and display the top N most frequent words.
10. Term Frequency-Inverse Document Frequency (TF-IDF): Implement TF-IDF to measure the importance of words in a document corpus.
11. Word Embeddings: Use pre-trained word embeddings (like Word2Vec or GloVe) to find similar words or phrases.

12. Text Similarity: Measure the similarity between two texts using techniques like cosine similarity or Jaccard similarity.
13. Text Summarization: Build an extractive text summarizer that extracts key sentences from a document.
14. Topic Modeling: Use Latent Dirichlet Allocation (LDA) or Non-Negative Matrix Factorization (NMF) to discover topics in a corpus.
15. Named Entity Recognition (NER): Implement a custom NER system using spaCy or NLTK.
16. Dependency Parsing: Parse sentences to identify the grammatical structure and dependencies between words.
17. Coreference Resolution: Resolve coreferences in text to determine which words or phrases refer to the same entities.
18. Text Generation: Build a simple text generator using Markov Chains or Recurrent Neural Networks (RNNs).
19. Language Modeling: Train a language model to predict the next word in a sequence of text.
20. Question Answering: Build a basic QA system that answers questions based on a corpus of text.
21. Text Classification with Deep Learning: Use TensorFlow or PyTorch to build a deep learning model for text classification.
22. Named Entity Recognition (NER) with Deep Learning: Implement a deep learning model (such as BiLSTM-CRF) for NER.

23. Sequence-to-Sequence Models: Build a sequence-to-sequence model for tasks like text summarization or translation.
24. BERT and Transformers: Fine-tune BERT or other Transformer models on a specific NLP task (e.g., sentiment analysis).
25. Cross-lingual NLP: Experiment with NLP tasks on multilingual datasets, using translation or language-specific models.
26. Text Clustering: Cluster similar documents together using algorithms like K-means clustering.
27. Dependency Parsing Visualization: Visualize the parsed dependencies of a sentence using spaCy or NLTK.
28. Text Data Cleaning: Implement text cleaning techniques like removing special characters, handling case sensitivity, etc.
29. Named Entity Recognition Evaluation: Evaluate the performance of an NER model using precision, recall, and F1-score.
30. Text Classification Evaluation: Evaluate the performance of a text classifier using metrics like accuracy, precision, recall, and F1-score.
31. Language Detection: Build a language detection system to identify the language of a given text.
32. Text Annotation: Annotate a dataset for sentiment, named entities, or other tasks to prepare it for training models.

33. Text Normalization: Normalize text by converting numbers to words, expanding contractions, etc.
34. Text Augmentation: Augment text data by adding synonyms, paraphrasing, or generating similar sentences.
35. Aspect-Based Sentiment Analysis: Analyze sentiments towards specific aspects or entities mentioned in reviews or articles.
36. Text to Speech Conversion: Convert text into speech using TTS libraries like pyttsx3 or gTTS.
37. Speech to Text Conversion: Convert speech audio into text using libraries like SpeechRecognition or Google Cloud Speech-to-Text.
38. Text Annotation Tools: Explore tools like Label Studio or Prodigy for efficient text annotation and labeling.
39. Text Generation with GPT-3: Experiment with OpenAI's GPT-3 for text generation tasks.
40. BERT-based Text Classification: Fine-tune BERT for text classification tasks on specialized datasets.
41. Textual Entailment: Build a system to determine if one text logically entails another (NLI tasks).
42. Text Masking: Implement text masking techniques for privacy protection or data anonymization.
43. Sentiment Analysis on Social Media: Analyze sentiment from Twitter or Reddit data using APIs and NLP libraries.

44. Text Generation with Transformers: Build a text generation model using transformer architectures like GPT-2 or GPT-3.
45. Named Entity Recognition on Biomedical Text: Adapt NER models to recognize entities in biomedical or scientific literature.
46. Text Classification for Fake News Detection: Build a classifier to detect fake news articles from genuine ones.
47. Aspect Extraction: Extract specific aspects or features mentioned in product reviews or customer feedback.
48. Textual Similarity for Duplicate Detection: Implement methods to detect duplicate or highly similar texts in a dataset.
49. Text Classification with CNNs: Use Convolutional Neural Networks (CNNs) for text classification tasks.
50. Textual Entailment with Transformer Models: Use transformer-based models like BERT or RoBERTa for textual entailment tasks.

-------------------- *End of chapter 9* --------------------

10 Common Terms

Natural Language Processing (NLP)

1. **Tokenization:** The process of breaking down text into smaller units (tokens), such as words or phrases.
2. **Stopwords:** Commonly used words (e.g., "and", "the") that are often filtered out during NLP tasks.
3. **Stemming:** Reducing words to their root form by removing suffixes or prefixes.
4. **Lemmatization:** Converting words to their base or dictionary form, considering the context.
5. **Part-of-Speech (POS) Tagging:** Assigning grammatical categories (e.g., noun, verb) to words in a sentence.
6. **Named Entity Recognition (NER):** Identifying and classifying named entities (e.g., names of persons, organizations) in text.
7. **Dependency Parsing:** Analyzing the grammatical structure of a sentence to determine relationships between words.
8. **Coreference Resolution:** Identifying which words or phrases refer to the same entities in a text.
9. **TF-IDF (Term Frequency-Inverse Document Frequency):** A statistical measure used to evaluate the importance of a word in a document relative to a corpus.

10. **Word Embeddings:** Mapping words or phrases to vectors of real numbers to capture semantic meanings.
11. **Language Modeling:** Predicting the probability of a sequence of words appearing in a language.
12. **Text Classification:** Assigning predefined categories or labels to text documents.
13. **Sentiment Analysis:** Determining the sentiment expressed in a text (e.g., positive, negative, neutral).
14. **Text Summarization:** Generating a concise summary of a longer text while retaining its key points.
15. **Topic Modeling:** Identifying topics or themes within a collection of documents.

Machine Learning (ML)

1. **Supervised Learning:** Training a model using labeled data to predict outcomes for new data.
2. **Unsupervised Learning:** Training a model on unlabeled data to discover patterns or structures.
3. **Reinforcement Learning:** Learning through trial and error based on feedback from actions taken in an environment.
4. **Overfitting:** When a model learns to perform well on training data but fails to generalize to new data.
5. **Underfitting:** When a model is too simple to capture the underlying patterns in the data.

6. **Bias-Variance Trade-off:** Balancing the error introduced by underfitting (bias) and overfitting (variance).
7. **Feature Engineering:** Creating new features or representations from raw data to improve model performance.
8. **Cross-validation:** Evaluating model performance by splitting data into multiple subsets for training and testing.
9. **Hyperparameters:** Parameters that control the learning process, set before training (e.g., learning rate, number of layers).
10. **Gradient Descent:** An optimization algorithm used to minimize the loss function and update model parameters.
11. **Regularization:** Techniques used to prevent overfitting by penalizing large model parameters.
12. **Ensemble Learning:** Combining multiple models to improve prediction accuracy or robustness.

Deep Learning (DL)

1. **Neural Network:** A network of interconnected artificial neurons (nodes) inspired by biological neural networks.
2. **Convolutional Neural Network (CNN):** A type of neural network designed for processing grid-like data (e.g., images).

3. **Recurrent Neural Network (RNN):** A type of neural network designed for sequential data, with connections between units forming a directed cycle.
4. **Long Short-Term Memory (LSTM):** A type of RNN designed to capture long-term dependencies in sequential data.
5. **Autoencoder:** A neural network trained to reproduce its input, used for unsupervised learning and dimensionality reduction.
6. **Generative Adversarial Network (GAN):** A framework for training two neural networks (generator and discriminator) in competition with each other.
7. **Transfer Learning:** Using knowledge gained from solving one problem to help solve a different, but related problem.
8. **Attention Mechanism:** Mechanism used in sequence-to-sequence models to focus on specific parts of input data.
9. **Batch Normalization:** Technique to improve the training speed and stability of neural networks by normalizing input batches.

Artificial Intelligence (AI)

1. **Artificial Intelligence:** The simulation of human intelligence by machines, typically through learning, reasoning, and problem-solving.

2. **Machine Intelligence:** The capability of a machine to imitate intelligent human behavior.
3. **Strong AI:** AI capable of performing any intellectual task that a human can.
4. **Weak AI (Narrow AI):** AI designed and trained for a specific task or set of tasks.
5. **AI Ethics:** The study of ethical issues arising from the development and deployment of AI systems.
6. **AI Bias:** Biases in AI systems resulting from data, algorithms, or their implementation, leading to unfair or discriminatory outcomes.

These definitions cover a wide range of concepts commonly encountered in NLP, ML, DL, and AI, providing a foundational understanding of the terminology used in these fields.

11 Common Python Libraries

1. Data Manipulation and Analysis:
    a. Pandas
    b. NumPy
    c. SciPy
    d. Dask
2. Machine Learning and AI:
    a. TensorFlow
    b. PyTorch
    c. Scikit-learn
    d. Keras
3. Data Visualization:
    a. Matplotlib
    b. Seaborn
    c. Plotly
    d. Web Development:
    e. Django
    f. Flask
    g. BeautifulSoup
4. GUI Development:
    a. Tkinter
    b. PyQt
5. Natural Language Processing:
    a. NLTK

   b. SpaCy
   c. Gensim
6. Database Access:
   a. SQLAlchemy
   b. psycopg2 (for PostgreSQL)
   c. pymongo (for MongoDB)
7. Web Scraping:
   a. Requests
   b. Scrapy
8. Testing:
   a. pytest
   b. unittest
9. Image Processing:
   a. OpenCV
   b. Pillow

-------------------- *End of chapter 11* --------------------

12 Hundred Comprehensive Questions on NLP

Introduction to NLP

1. What is Natural Language Processing (NLP)?
2. Why is NLP important in today's technological landscape?
3. How is NLP used in everyday applications?
4. Trace the evolution of NLP over the years.
5. What are the future trends and challenges in NLP?

Fundamental Concepts of Text PreProcessing

6. Define Text PreProcessing and its significance in NLP.
7. Describe the process of text acquisition in NLP.
8. What is tokenization? Why is it important in NLP?
9. How does stop words removal contribute to text preprocessing?
10. Compare stemming and lemmatization in NLP.
11. Explain the concept of Part-of-Speech (POS) tagging.
12. What is Named Entity Recognition (NER) and its applications?
13. How does normalization contribute to text preprocessing?
14. Discuss techniques for junk data removal in NLP.
15. What role does spell checking and correction play in text preprocessing?
16. How is noise reduction achieved in NLP?
17. Compare different methods of encoding and vectorization in NLP.

18. Explain the concept of One-Hot Encoding and its limitations.
19. What are Word Embeddings? How are they used in NLP?
20. How does TF-IDF vectorization work in NLP?

Statistical Methods in NLP

21. Introduce the role of probability and statistics in NLP.
22. Explain the application of probability in NLP.
23. Discuss statistical techniques commonly used in NLP.
24. What is TF-IDF and how is it calculated in NLP?
25. Compare Word2Vec, GloVe, and FastText in NLP.
26. Describe the architecture and training process of Word2Vec.
27. How does BERT improve upon previous NLP models?
28. What are the key features of the GPT model in NLP?
29. Explain the concept of XLNet and its advantages in NLP.

Machine Learning Basics

30. What are the different types of machine learning algorithms?
31. Explain supervised learning and give examples relevant to NLP.
32. Discuss the principles of unsupervised learning in NLP.
33. How does semi-supervised learning apply to NLP tasks?
34. Describe reinforcement learning and its applications in NLP.
35. Explain the working principle of Logistic Regression.
36. How does Support Vector Machine (SVM) classify text data?
37. Discuss the Naive Bayes classifier and its assumptions.

38. Explain the decision-making process in Decision Trees.
39. What are the advantages of Random Forest in NLP tasks?
40. How does K-Nearest Neighbours (KNN) work in text classification?
41. Compare different binary classifiers used in NLP.
42. How are multi-class classifiers implemented in NLP?

Deep Learning for NLP

43. Introduce Neural Networks and their relevance to NLP.
44. Explain the architecture of Recurrent Neural Networks (RNNs) in NLP.
45. How does Long Short-Term Memory (LSTM) improve upon RNNs?
46. Describe the application of Convolutional Neural Networks (CNNs) in NLP.
47. What are Sequence-to-Sequence models and their use cases?
48. Explain the concept of Transfer Learning in NLP.
49. What are the common evaluation metrics used in NLP tasks?
50. Discuss real-world applications of Deep Learning in NLP.
51. What are the major challenges faced in applying Deep Learning to NLP?
52. What future directions are anticipated in Deep Learning for NLP?

Practical Applications

53. Describe methodologies used in sentiment analysis.
54. How is sentiment analysis applied in real-world scenarios?

55. Analyze Twitter sentiment using NLP techniques.
56. How does NLP help in customer review analysis?
57. Explain the process of text classification in NLP.
58. What are the key differences between binary and multi-class classification?
59. How is Named Entity Recognition (NER) implemented in practical applications?

Ethical Considerations in NLP

60. Discuss the concept of bias in NLP algorithms.
61. How can fairness be ensured in NLP applications?
62. What are the privacy concerns associated with NLP and how can they be addressed?
63. Explain the importance of data protection in NLP.

General Questions

64. How can NLP techniques be used to enhance search engine functionalities?
65. Discuss the role of NLP in automated summarization of text.
66. How does NLP contribute to machine translation systems?
67. Explain the challenges of sentiment analysis on social media data.
68. How can NLP help in detecting fake news and misinformation?
69. Describe the role of NLP in chatbot development.
70. What are the ethical implications of using NLP in surveillance systems?

71. Compare traditional rule-based NLP systems with modern machine learning-based approaches.
72. How does context affect the performance of NLP models?
73. Discuss the impact of domain-specific language on NLP tasks.
74. Explain the limitations of current NLP models in understanding sarcasm and humor.
75. How can NLP models handle languages with complex grammatical structures?
76. Describe the steps involved in building a named entity recognition system.
77. What are the advantages and disadvantages of using pre-trained language models in NLP?
78. Discuss the role of attention mechanisms in improving NLP tasks.
79. How does data preprocessing affect the performance of NLP models?
80. Explain the concept of adversarial attacks in NLP.
81. What measures can be taken to improve the interpretability of NLP models?
82. How can NLP be used in healthcare applications such as clinical text analysis?
83. Discuss the potential biases introduced by training data in NLP applications.

84. How does the size of training data impact the performance of NLP models?
85. Explain the concept of semantic similarity in NLP and its applications.
86. Describe the challenges in creating multilingual NLP systems.
87. How can NLP techniques be applied to enhance accessibility for differently-abled individuals?
88. Discuss the role of NLP in analyzing trends and sentiments in financial markets.
89. What are the ethical considerations when using NLP for content moderation?
90. How does cross-lingual NLP facilitate global communication?
91. Explain the concept of domain adaptation in NLP.
92. Discuss the implications of using NLP in personalized advertising.
93. How can NLP models be deployed efficiently in real-time applications?
94. What are the challenges of scaling NLP models to process large volumes of data?
95. Describe the role of data annotation in training NLP models.
96. How does NLP contribute to improving search relevance in e-commerce platforms?

97. Discuss the role of interpretability in gaining trust in NLP applications.
98. What are the computational challenges of training deep learning models for NLP?
99. How can NLP techniques be used for summarizing legal documents?
100. Describe the steps involved in developing a language translation system using NLP.

------------------- *End of chapter 12* -------------------

Thank You

www.ingramcontent.com/pod-product-compliance
Lightning Source LLC
LaVergne TN
LVHW021148160826
845679LV00024B/2083

* 9 7 9 8 8 9 4 9 8 5 5 0 3 *